ROSE TO REVIVAL

An Unlikely Beginning to an Extraordinary Ending

Tonya Prewett

TRILOGY CHRISTIAN PUBLISHERS
Tustin, CA

Trilogy Christian Publishers
A Wholly Owned Subsidiary of Trinity Broadcasting Network
2442 Michelle Drive
Tustin, CA 92780

Roses to Revival

Copyright © 2025 by Tonya Prewett

All Scripture quotations, unless otherwise noted, are taken from THE HOLY BIBLE, NEW INTERNATIONAL VERSION®, NIV® Copyright © 1973, 1978, 1984, 2011 by Biblica, Inc.® Used by permission. All rights reserved worldwide.

Scripture quotations marked ESV are taken from the ESV® Bible (The Holy Bible, English Standard Version®), copyright © 2001 by Crossway Bibles, a publishing ministry of Good News Publishers. Used by permission. All rights reserved.

Scripture quotations marked TPT are from The Passion Translation®. Copyright © 2017, 2018, 2020 by Passion & Fire Ministries, Inc. Used by permission. All rights reserved. ThePassionTranslation.com.

All rights reserved, including the right to reproduce this book or portions thereof in any form whatsoever.

For information, address Trilogy Christian Publishing
Rights Department, 2442 Michelle Drive, Tustin, CA 92780.

Trilogy Christian Publishing/ TBN and colophon are trademarks of Trinity Broadcasting Network.

For information about special discounts for bulk purchases, please contact Trilogy Christian Publishing.

Trilogy Disclaimer: The views and content expressed in this book are those of the author and may not necessarily reflect the views and doctrine of Trilogy Christian Publishing or the Trinity Broadcasting Network.

10 9 8 7 6 5 4 3 2 1

Library of Congress Cataloging-in-Publication Data is available.

ISBN 979-8-89597-500-8

ISBN 979-8-89597-501-5 (ebook)

Dedication

To my family, Chad, Madison, Mallory, Mary Mykal, Grant and Hosanna Rose,

What an incredible journey we have been on! Thank you for always being by my side, for your continuous prayers, and for cheering me on every step of the way. I would not want to do any of it without you.

Endorsements

I've watched Tonya Prewett pour her life into reaching this generation, and I've seen firsthand the fire God has lit through her obedience. Roses to Revival isn't just a book—it's a call to surrender, trust God with your hardest moments, and step into the revival He's already stirring.

Jennie Allen
Founder and Visionary of IF:Gathering and Gather25

In a world where prayers are often whispered with hesitation, Tonya Prewett reminds us to pray boldly, believing that God is able to do more than we can ask or imagine. Roses to Revival is a testimony of faith in action—of stepping out, trusting big, and watching God move in ways only He can. Through personal stories of obedience and answered prayers, this book will challenge you to stop praying safe, predictable prayers and start asking for the impossible.

Jonathan Pokluda
Lead Pastor of Harris Creek Baptist Church, Best-selling author, Host of *Becoming Something* podcast

It has been amazing to watch a move of God spread across college campuses as Tonya Prewett consistently said "yes" to making a way. Be inspired by her story of faith and obedience, Roses to Revival captures the power of what a big God can do with big prayers. A generation meets Jesus.

Lisa Bevere
NYT Bestselling Author, Speaker, and Co-Founder of Messenger International

When I think about the last 5-6 years of our lives, I am blown away by how God has rewarded Tonya's faithfulness. From the highest of highs to the lowest of lows I have witnessed her unwavering pursuit of her God. I have had a front row seat to watch Tonya go from being an incredible mom to our 3 girls to God allowing her to become a mom to this entire generation. God is using this mighty prayer warrior in ways that cannot be explained and He has anointed her ... "for such a time as this"

Chad Prewett
Auburn Mens' Basketball Assistant Coach, Tonya's husband

Tonya is a world changer and leader in revival. This book is going to bless you and show you that no matter who you are or where you are in life, God can use you in mighty ways! You just need to say yes to Him. I know this book is going to encourage you to take your first step!

Jeanine Amapola Ward
Christian influencer, author, podcast host

Tonya Prewett, (My Mama Prew), lives her life with a God-confident urgency and an unceasing fervor for MORE of the presence of God, obedience to His word, and witnessing His kingdom come for an entire generation. She will not sit on the sidelines like the enemy wanted... Her fervor and fire, passion and purpose, and ultimate "YES" to God has made echoes and ripples in the waves of eternity. This book, filled with moments, trials, breakthrough's, and hope isn't just a testimony of God's goodness- It's a commission and call to live the life you were ultimately created for! Buckle up.

Grant Troutt
Speaker and Pastor, Tonya's Son-in-Law

Foreword

I remember the day I sat in my car, crying in the garage, wondering if God still saw me. I was in a wilderness and waiting season. I knew God had more for me but I felt behind in life and overlooked. In that moment of desperation, I did what I've always done—I called my mom.

What I didn't know then was that she had been praying bold, behind-the-scenes prayers for me—prayers that would launch me into the wildest, most unlikely journey of my life. Her voice on the other end of the phone was steady and Spirit-filled: "God hasn't forgotten you. He's preparing you. Get up and start writing."

So I did.

What unfolded next wasn't just my story—it was ours. And more than that, it was God's. A journey from roses to revival.

If you had told my mom years ago that she would one day lead a nationwide revival, speak in packed-out arenas, and watch thousands of students give their lives to Jesus because of her 'yes' to God... she probably would've laughed—or cried.

My mom's story didn't start with a microphone or a ministry. It started with hidden prayer walks and quiet faithfulness. It started with early mornings of making school lunches, cheering on my dad from the stands as he chased his coaching dreams, and showing up for me and my sisters in every single season—through heartbreak, confusion, and unexpected platforms. It started with leading a college girls small group and hearing the pain, sin, and confusion that weighed them down.

This book is a front-row seat to the miracles that happen when you say 'yes' to God—even when it's scary, even when it doesn't make sense. It's a story of what happens when a woman gets on her knees before God for hours a day, when she walks University campuses praying for students, and neighborhood sidewalks interceding for the nation, and when she believes God for something so big only He can do it.

This is my mom's story—but it's also a call to all of us.

A call to the secret place.

A call to pray bold prayers that feel too big.

A call to forgive so we can truly live.

A call to trust God in the middle of the waiting, the hard, and the hidden.

A call to step out in purpose.

A call to believe that the same Spirit that raised Jesus from the dead is still moving in power right now.

Revival isn't a thing of the past or some far-off dream—it's happening here. Now. In our generation. On our college campuses. And it doesn't just start in arenas, it starts in our hearts and on our knees. It starts in living rooms and prayer walks.

If you've ever wondered if God could use your ordinary, broken, unlikely life to do something eternal—this book will shout a resounding yes.

It's a message that reminds you that you don't have to be the most qualified, the most visible, or the most ready. You just have to be willing. It's a story for anyone who's tired of playing it safe and is ready to pray bigger, believe deeper, and be part of something greater than themselves.

So read with expectancy.

Let this book stir something in you. Let it wake you up. Let it drive you to your knees. Let it create a conviction to rise up and live on purpose. Let it remind you that our time on earth is short and we have work to do. Let it empower you to believe for greater miracles, because God isn't done with you yet, in fact, He's just getting started.

Because like my mom reminds us in this book, revival isn't just coming—it's here.

—Madison Prewett Troutt

Contents

Chapter 1. Don't Pray Short 1

Chapter 2. The Journey to the Roses 6

Chapter 3. Revival 40

Chapter 4. Learn to Forgive So You Fulfill Your
    Destiny 99

Chapter 5. Your Esther Moment 107

Chapter 6. See Me 121

Chapter 7. Step Into Your Purpose............................. 130

Chapter 8. Pain to Purpose 136

Chapter 9. The Power of Prayer.................................. 142

Chapter 10. The King Is Coming! 146

Afterword 150

Endnotes 151

CHAPTER 1

Don't Pray Short

"Something BIG is coming!"

I was going through a long list of emails at work when this heading popped off the page and grabbed my attention. I read it over and over and made a mental note to never delete this email. It was from an apparel company, and I never even bothered to read the email through. But for the next few weeks I looked at that subject line every single day: "Something Big Is Coming!"

I felt myself getting unsettled in my job. At the time, I was the Director of Development for a private school in Auburn, Alabama. I would go into work and pull up that email and read the subject line. Over and over. Then dread the rest of the day. It was as if I knew I could not stay in that job any longer. Like God was saying, "Something BIG is coming...don't miss it!" The strong sense of being unsettled led to an enormous amount of pressure and tension. I remember leaving dinner with my husband one night when he pulled the car into a mall parking lot and said, "What's going on? You seem stressed and not yourself lately." I explained that I felt it was time to resign from my job because God was telling me that something BIG was coming. He responded, "Go turn in your resignation tomorrow." So, I did.

What happens over the next five years of my life is simply miraculous.

After resigning from my job in 2018, I devoted my days to prayer. I would walk Auburn University's campus, our neighborhood, or the stairs in our home for hours every day and pray. My main prayer in that particular season was for the Auburn University men's basketball team to make it to the Final Four. My husband is an assistant basketball coach at Auburn University but previously was head coach at a local private school. When Auburn hired a new head basketball coach, Bruce Pearl, I started praying every day that Coach Pearl could not go anywhere that he didn't hear my husband's name. One day, out of the blue, my husband got a phone call. "Hey, Coach Prewett...this is Coach Bruce Pearl. I don't have a position, but I cannot go anywhere that I do not hear your name. Can you come in and talk to me?" The next week my husband went to meet with Coach Pearl and left with a D1 coaching position. Prayer works.

Fast forward to the 2018 basketball season, and I'm praying every day, "God, help our team to make it to a Final Four." The thing is our team was just average. We were not a Final Four team. But I kept praying.

I often listen to Pastor Craig Groeschel's messages when on a walk. I was so encouraged by his story of how his wife, Amy, prays bold prayers—prayers that could only be a result of God's mighty hand. I decided that year I would believe for bigger, God-sized goals. One of those prayers was for Auburn Men's Basketball to make it to the Final Four. In my mind, I thought this was impossible and would only be achieved if God intervened. I prayed it every day. As our team began to play in March Madness, first in the SEC tournament and then the NCAA tournament, miraculous things began to happen. We could not lose. SEC champs, first round of NCAA, Sweet Sixteen, Elite Eight, and then—The Final Four. What! I kept saying, "GOD! You heard my prayers! Thank You for hearing my prayers!"

If you watched that Final Four game, you know Auburn was down by ten points going into the final two minutes of the game. I left my seat, went upstairs, and began to pace and pray. I prayed for a miracle. Slowly but surely, we came back point by point until we gained a lead of two with less than a minute left in the game. It's the opponent's ball and the clock is winding down. Only seconds left and our fans are on their feet screaming and chanting the War Eagle chants! With seven seconds left on the clock, one of our players fouls one of their players as he's shooting a three-point shot. The arena is silent as we all hold our breath. "Just miss one. Just miss one," I kept thinking as we waited for what seemed like hours. First shot goes up, he makes it. Second shot goes up, he makes it. Third shot goes up, he makes it. The time runs out on the game clock, and we lose the game by one point. *One.* Why God? Why would you bring us this far to let us lose by one point in the last seconds of the game? I did not understand.

The players, coaches, and families made their way to the plane to head home. No one spoke. The overwhelming feeling of defeat left us all speechless. As I sat there on the plane, questioning God, asking over and over, "Why?" I heard Him say, "I would have given you a national championship, but you prayed short. You only prayed for a Final Four."

As I reflected on the game and looked back over the miraculous finish to our season, I realized something. Even though I prayed big, I still prayed too small. What a lesson! God is powerful and almighty—He is not limited in what He can do! I do not ever want my faith to be limited by my small thinking. I received what I asked for. If only I had trusted for more. A Final Four is huge, but a national championship is the ultimate achievement. I will not accept good when I can have great. Nothing is impossible with my God!

Believe for something so big that it can only happen if God does it. That has always been my motto in life. And it pretty much sums up the last five years of my life. Let me take you on that journey.

Takeaways:

- Pray big prayers, expect big results.
- Why not pray for something so big that it can only happen if God does it?
- Nothing is impossible with God.

CHAPTER 2

The Journey to the Roses

In the spring of 2019 (knowing our oldest daughter, Madison, had been struggling in some areas), my husband and I decided to call our pastor and ask him to pray specifically for her. He encouraged us, prayed with us, and left us with a strong statement. "We are going to pray and agree that in the next thirty days Madison will receive a breakthrough. God will shift something in her life and open new doors." He continued, "Over the next thirty days we will celebrate Easter (the Resurrection) and we will believe for a resurrection in Madison's life. A new beginning." So, we began to pray.

During the next few weeks, Madison seemed to go through one of the toughest spiritual battles she had ever experienced. She started questioning if she even had a purpose in life. It was the lowest I had ever seen her. She went from being in a serious relationship for four years with the guy she thought she would marry, surrounded by the strongest community of friends, to being single and working in a job away from home where she never saw anyone. It seemed everyone around her was living their best life and she was camping in the valley. Madison is a very relational person, but she found herself in a season of loneliness and depression.

One particular day she came in from a work meeting and just hit her lowest point. She pulled into the garage and started crying. She asked God if He could hear her. If He saw her. Or even cared about her. As she was crying and praying, she called me. She said, "MOM! God doesn't see me anymore. He has forgotten me!" I wanted to feel sorry for her, but something rose up inside of me. I said, "Madison, God has not forgotten you! God is preparing you for something bigger that is coming. You will write books and speak to women and girls all over the world. Get up and go inside your apartment and start writing your book!"

As soon as we hung up the phone, Madison went inside her apartment, took out her computer, and started writing. While she was writing, a friend sent her a text. "Hey, Madison. You are on my mind, and I wanted to share this word with you." The person who sent the message had no idea what was going on in her life, but when Madison clicked the link and started to read, she felt as if God Himself was speaking directly to her. Now I see this was for far more than we could have ever imagined. One step of obedience leading to greater things to come! Below is the message Madi was sent. Although it's long, I believe God has a message in it for you, even today!

> *There is a resounding sound from heaven being thundered: "WILL YOU TRUST ME AND MY DIRECTION?"*
>
> *There is a MASSIVE change taking place right now; there is HUGE momentum and acceleration happening, and some of the greatest alignments by the hand of God are happening RIGHT NOW. But we cannot enter into all the new things God is doing if we are not yielded to His ways.*
>
> *The Lord is asking the question, "Will you trust Me and My direction?" not "Will you rely on your own direction or the direction of yesterday." It is imperative right now, as God's people, that we are ACTIVELY and INTENTIONALLY asking for the wisdom of God and the directions that He is leading.*
>
> *The Lord showed me that some of the directions that He was leading His people into in this new era were completely unexpected. Many were shocked, stunned, and slightly perplexed in the direction of the Lord because it is SO unexpected.*

As this was happening, I saw the invitation from the Lord to RADICALLY TRUST. As God's people abandoned themselves completely to the Lord, His direction in obedience, that ONE MOMENT of radical obedience in the direction He was leading CHANGED EVERYTHING. I watched in this vision as a whole new world opened up before them. I watched the divine RIPPLE EFFECT that took place from that ONE DECISION to follow Jesus and the leading of the Holy Spirit in His direction, as it not only opened up NUMEROUS NEW DIRECTIONS but also a level of INCREASE that had never been experienced before.

This will be THE GREATEST TEST OF TRUST!

This will be the test of trust where EVERYTHING is being "put on the line in faith" before the Lord. It is the kind of trust that throws EVERYTHING upon the Lord, the deepest yieldedness that many have ever experienced. Many in the body of Christ are feeling their soul react to this place of deep yielding. There's been fear, there's been anxiety, there's been stress, but IN that place where the Lord is asking FOR EVERYTHING, the resounding of the Lord's heart "COME FOLLOW ME" meeting with the resounding "YES, LORD" from His people is dealing with ROOTS of fear, anxiety, stress, fear of man, intimidation, doubt, and unbelief "ONCE AND FOR ALL."

This is the greatest test of trust for many of you, but can I encourage you, in this place of the greatest test of trust, you are about to encounter the deepest level of the revelation of who He is and His faithfulness in your life. In the "new directions" that He is leading, in this place of "come follow Me" even if you're scared, even if you don't understand and it looks different to what you expect, "you are going to receive the greatest gift of all—seeing Me like you have never seen Me before."

The enemy and fear are screaming, "What if this happens?" Or "This is going to happen if you step out...." All of these whispers being negative...where I hear the Lord's whisper, "I've gone before you. I've got you covered, and you are stepping into a realm of grace and demonstration of My power unlike anything you have ever seen." (This is profound for what all is coming—Exodus 33!)

HARVEST IS COMING IN UNEXPECTED PACKAGES. (This! We had no idea what was ahead!)

I then heard the words, "Harvest is coming in unexpected packages." These directions the Lord is leading His people in are actually the "pinnacle of harvest" thus far. What God is about to do, how He is going to increase you, the flourishing of the seeds that is going to explode, the promises of God that are going to manifest—it is going to take place in EVERY DIRECTION. This explosion of harvest in your life is going to be the greatest manifestation of harvest in your life thus far.

*Can you not discern this new day of destiny
breaking forth around you?
The early signs of my purposes and plans
are bursting forth.
The budding vines of new life
are now blooming everywhere.
The fragrance of their flowers whispers,
"There is change in the air."
– Song of Songs 2:13 (TPT)*

Not only is the Lord bursting harvest IN your life in unexpected packages through these new directions of His hand, He is preparing you in the radical place of TRUSTING HIM for the MIGHTY HARVEST OF SOULS upon the earth. God is uprooting things in the heart through this great test of trust and exploding His truth within you to PREPARE YOU to move into the next level of your destiny and divine positioning that will take place to see MANY SOULS come into the Kingdom. The "next level" of your destiny for many is in the AWAKENING of who you are and who He is and going forth no longer held back by fear, fear of man, people-pleasing, doubt, and unbelief, and in the recognition and awakening of who you are, you shift atmospheres and extend the Kingdom wherever you go.

You must follow Me wherever I lead and however "out of the box" or "unexpected" it looks. (Wow again for what's coming!)

Some of you have been feeling anxiety, fear, etc. about a pathway the Lord is leading, but He wants you to know to not fear, for He is with you; there is nothing to fear. This is a point of major encounter with Him, a great test of trust where the revelation of His truth and faithfulness will change your life, and the "domino effect" of His acceleration that will take place through your obedience will be like nothing you have ever seen. He's got you covered!

I saw many feeling anxious. "If I go this way, it's so against what I expected or against the grain, it seems like a backwards step," and I heard the Lord say, "This step is actually your greatest step into divine acceleration that you have ever experienced."

God is shifting! God is changing! God is reshaping! Follow His voice, follow His direction. He's with you and will not leave you, and you will see great miracles explode in your obedience to Him. It may be the greatest test of trust and at times super painful, but you're actually being positioned for the greatest encounters and breakthroughs of your life, but be INTENTIONAL to continue to ask for His wisdom and to know His ways and then follow Him, and that is the place of tremendous peace and joy![1]

On May 10, twenty-nine days later, Madison got a call from ABC's *The Bachelor*. They told her they were interested in her being on the show and would like for her to interview for their next season. Madison laughed. "I'm sorry, but you must have the wrong Madison. I'm going to marry a pastor, and I didn't apply for your show." They went on to explain that someone else had sent in an application for her and they were very interested in her being on their show. She hung up the phone and called me. "Mommmm, ABC's *The Bachelor* just called me and said they want me to interview for their show. I would NEVER!"

My response to her shocked even me—it had to be God! I said, "Madison, we do not close a door until we pray. If God wants you to take this very unlikely path, then we will trust it. If not, He will close the door."

The process began with a request to send in photos and a video. Madison and I went to the Auburn arena and created a video. I must say we did a great job! I told Madison after creating the video that the producers would probably flag her as a top contender.

After a month or so, Madison received another call from one of the *Bachelor* producers saying that they would like for her to come to Atlanta for an interview. On July 14, I drove Madison to her interview. She interviewed with four producers and said it went extremely well. She loved it.

I have never been a "sign" person, but I have to tell you the "signs" over the next few months as we prayed so fervently about Madi going on the show were undeniable. I left Atlanta and went on a trip to Dallas. When I ordered room service, the food was delivered with a single red rose.

The next week I took my youngest daughter on a trip to tour a university, and on the way, there was the largest sign on the side of the road with neon letters that said, "Roses, roses, roses!"

A week later, I went to Atlanta for an appointment. The parking spaces were all taken, so I had to park at a nearby shop. I had some time to spare, so I was responding to text messages. A man in the car beside me was waving me down and blowing his horn. I ignored him for a while, thinking he was hitting on me. But he would not stop waving at me. When I gave him my attention, he smiled and pointed at the shop in front of me. Then he drove off. I was shocked to see the window of the shop had a huge mural of a hand holding a single red rose.

The next week, my husband and I went on a couple's trip to Cabo. On the second day of our trip, I mentioned to the other ladies that I would like to watch *The Bachelorette* that night, so we would need to plan dinner earlier than usual, which led me to explaining to our friends that Madi was interviewing for *The Bachelor*.

While lying out on the beach that day, a lady noticed my beach bag and asked where I got it. We started talking, and I asked where she was from. She said, Los Angeles. I told her that my daughter and I took a trip there and went on *The Price is Right*, where she'd won $8000. She suggested that we should go on the *Ellen* show. I told her that we'd tried on our last trip, but it was sold out. She shared that it usually sells out quickly, and the only way she was able to go was because her friend is a producer in LA. I asked, "Oh, really? Who is your friend a producer for?" She said, "*The Bachelor*." I'm sure my eyes got really big, and I sat there shocked for a second. I said, "That's crazy! My daughter is interviewing to be a contestant on the show."

We watched the show that night. The next morning, my friends went out to the beach early. They called me and said, "You need to get down to the beach right now." So, I rushed down to the beach. On the sand someone had painted a giant single red rose! Later that evening, our butler came into our room with a vase and a single red rose. All this had my attention.

A few weeks later, Madison received another call from a producer saying they would like to fly her to LA for the finale weekend and a final interview. She flew to LA on August 5.

Madi interviewed with thirty producers in LA. She called me after the interview and told me she absolutely loved the producers. She said she wasn't sure if they would cast her but that it could not have gone any better.

Israel

On the same day, my husband and I left for a trip to Israel with several couples through JH Israel. While there, we visited many different locations and heard teachings from the leader of JH Israel at each destination. We began our trip at the Sea of Galilee. The hotel we stayed at overlooks the Sea of Galilee, and when we arrived at the hotel, there were red roses everywhere.

On day two, we went out to the sea for a teaching session by our team leader. We each found a place to stand or sit as she spoke. I sat with a couple of the ladies on a wooden bench. As I turned to set my journal down,

I noticed there was a large rose engraved on the back of the bench. This was starting to get weird. I pushed the thought aside and continued to listen to the amazing teaching.

A couple of days later, we visited the Garden of Gethsemane. The teaching was focused on Jesus praying in the garden and how He prayed for God to let the cup pass from Him. After the teaching, the leader gave us each a small wooden cup and asked us to break up and find a private place in the garden to pray. She told us to focus on one specific thing that we were believing God for. I chose to pray for Madison, for wisdom and direction, for her purpose and her future husband. I looked around the garden and found one spot that was not already occupied and took a seat on a log. I went to set my cup on the log and noticed that engraved on the log was a single rose. Was God really trying to show me multiple signs to give me peace about what was coming?

Being in Israel while my daughter was alone in LA interviewing with *Bachelor* producers was tough for this mama. I felt like I needed to be in two places at the same time. I anxiously awaited the call from Madison. When she did finally call, she told me all about the interview. How much she enjoyed it and loved everyone. Again, she mentioned that she did not know how it would all turn out, but it had been such a fun experience so far.

When I tell you I could not go anywhere in Israel without seeing a rose or the word rose, I am not exaggerating. Guys wearing ball caps would walk up to me with a single rose on their cap. Men wearing shirts that were covered in roses. Trash cans with roses and the word rose on them. Water bottles with roses on the labels. Jewelry with roses. Everywhere we went.

The next day, we visited the Pool of Bethesda. As our leader finished her teaching, she stopped and said, "I feel like we need to all pray for someone in the group." I didn't think much of it, but my hand went up. The team gathered around me and started praying. The prayers were very specific, even though they had no idea that Madison was interviewing for the show. Then one of the leaders walked up to me and said, "I see a ring of fire surrounding your family. God is going to protect you in what's coming." She had no idea!

Our next stop in Israel was Ariel in Samaria at the National Leadership Center, one of the highest points in the city. We had the best experience. My husband and I were able to plant a tree on this mountain. As we were digging the hole, I had the strongest feeling that we needed to write out our goals and dreams for our family and bury them beneath that tree. I found paper and a pen, and we wrote out our family dreams and goals. As we buried them, I prayed that as the tree grew in Israel, so would our family's dreams. As I reflect on that time, I'm so grateful for all God has done since then—can we stop and praise the Lord right now for what is coming!

On our last day in Israel, I received a call from Madison saying she had been chosen as a contestant on the show. This didn't surprise me one bit. I already knew and had peace. She would make it to the end.

The next few months flew by. Madison and I went shopping for all the things. Not knowing how long she would be there, she had to prepare for the full ten weeks. Rose ceremony dresses, casual outfits, date night outfits, sportswear, and then all the extras, just in case. They only allowed one large suitcase. Madi packed three!

41 Letters

When Madison accepted the invitation to be a contestant on the show, I was stricken with the realization that I would not be able to talk to her. We talked every day, so this was a serious issue for me. I knew I had to find a creative way to be able to talk to her since I could not pick up the phone and call. So, I decided to write her letters. The problem was, I had no idea how long she would be gone. A day. A week. A month. Or longer. So, I just started writing. Every day leading up to her leaving, I would write several letters a day. When I got to letter number 41, I felt prompted to stop. It seemed weird to stop at 41, but I did. I tied a ribbon around the letters and gave them to Madison on the day she left. 41 letters. All numbered and bound with a red ribbon.

On September 16, we drove Madi to the airport and said our goodbyes. I handed Madison the stack of letters and told her that would be my way of talking to her while she was filming.

On October 26, Madison returned to Auburn for hometowns. This was the first time we saw her since she left for filming—exactly forty-one days later. Still blows my mind!

I could have never anticipated what those letters represented or how they would impact Madison while on the show. She told me later that there was a day when she packed her bags and decided she was leaving because she didn't think she could stay any longer. She wanted to walk away and give up, but she read my letter for that day, and it said, "Madi, remember when you ran track in high school? How, when you ran the 400m race, you would get to a point where you would want to give up and stop running? But you didn't quit, and you finished the race. Don't quit, Madi. God is not finished. Stay the course. Stay in the race."

This was exactly what she needed to give her the strength to keep going. And finish she did. Madi later shared her faith and stand for purity on national television to over ten million viewers. You will later see how this decision to stay in the race led to much more than Madi could have ever imagined in that moment.

While Madi was filming for the show, I spent most of my days praying all day. And night. I would literally get on the floor, face down, and pray for hours. My prayers were always asking God for three things: protection, favor, and wisdom.

There was one particular day when the stress of it all got the best of me. Not knowing if Madi was physically, mentally, or emotionally okay. Not knowing if she was being manipulated, blindsided, or misrepresented. My anxiety was so high I thought I was having a nervous breakdown. I got dressed to go to the hospital to ask them if they could put me to sleep. It sounds crazy, I know, but I felt like I could not physically cope. A friend texted me at that moment and asked me to come sit with her. I told her I would not come sit with her, or talk to her or anyone else for that matter—I was going to the hospital to see if they could do something to stop the pain.

When I got in my car, for some reason it took me to my friend's house. I had no intention of going there, but I did. Just talking to her helped me settle down. We didn't talk about Madi or the show, just small talk. She encouraged me to have my husband pray over me. I left there, drove to a nearby parking lot, and called my husband. He was in an important coaching meeting. I didn't care. I asked him to pray for me. He left the meeting and said a simple prayer for me. I left the lot and went to grab lunch. I listened to one of my favorite pastors preach a message on "Treasures in Darkness" while I ate.[2] It literally changed everything for me. It gave me clarity on why Madi was on that show. Below are my notes from that sermon:

> *God is the potter. Madi is the clay. He will give her treasures in darkness. He will give her hidden riches of secret places. God has stuff in places nobody knows. God has water in the earth that has been prepared for such a time as this. When God gets ready to bless you, it can come from every direction.*

> *When God gets ready to bless you, He can do it in the presence of your enemies. He can do it around witches and warlocks. He can bless you in any situation. HE IS GOD, AND BESIDES HIM THERE IS NO OTHER. NO ONE CAN TELL HIM WHAT TO DO. NO ONE CAN CHANGE HIM. HE WAS HERE BEFORE THE FOUNDATION OF THE WORLD. And He will be here for all of eternity! HE IS GOD!*

> *God does His best work in the dark. When God gets ready to put you in the light, He puts you through the dark. When a camera gets ready to develop film, it gets developed in the dark. You prayed for*

the light, but God is developing you in the dark. The season you are in is preparation for what God is getting ready to do in your life.

If you're going through darkness, God will move. He said, "Let there be light," and darkness RAN FROM THE LIGHT! Darkness cannot exist in the presence of light.

When God created the world, He started in the dark.

God's getting ready to pull something out of you that you didn't even know you had. I thought I was nothing. But God put me in a dark place, and I realized who I was.

Seeds have to be planted. In the privacy of darkness, seeds go through a metamorphosis that they couldn't go through in the light. God allows you to go through your changes in the darkness. The wrestling and struggling happen in the darkness before you enter the light.

Something BIG is about to happen! (A reminder!)

The power that is going to deliver you is coming from the inside.

Because Mary was willing to go through the gossip and almost losing her husband, she delivered what would deliver her. There is something in Madi that will deliver her. In order to produce it, she has to go through the dark place.

Sometimes it's about being in the right place at the right time. You didn't know you would meet someone who would change the trajectory of your life. You stumbled upon a treasure. A miracle. An answer. A new job. An opportunity. A husband. (Through this unlikely journey, a divine connection was made that led Madi to her husband!)

Paul gave up his eyesight for insight. His experience on the Damascus Road prepared him for what he would write later.

For all the people God could have used, He used someone who killed Christians. Your enemies have a purpose. He will make your enemies your footstool. Leave room for your enemies to change.

What God has for you is too big for you to be small. For you to hold grudges. For you to be petty. God can take someone who is about to kill you and use them to write the New Testament to feed you. People change. So, we need to let go and forgive.

God may use your enemies to bless you. Open your door to them.

A blessing is coming. A hidden treasure. The darkness you are in is a sign that the blessing is coming.

Planting and burial look the same. You dig up the earth, you put something in it, and you cover it up. When you bury it, you put something in it to stay. When you plant it, you cover it to change.

You have NOT BEEN BURIED. YOU HAVE BEEN PLANTED. You might have been in darkness, but you will sprout again. You will laugh again. A joyous laugh. You will dance again. In your own house. When you see what God brings up in your life after this. You will rejoice again. He's going to give you the treasure of darkness and the hidden secrets that have been hidden from everyone else.

God is present in trouble. He is there now, developing your next blessing. Your next season. Your next place of increase. Your overflow season. It's happening now. It shall come to pass. IT SHALL COME TO PASS.

There may be enemies around you. God has placed you out of reach. They can't defeat you. They can't keep you from your destiny. Remain confident. You may feel like you are surrounded by an army, but you are surrounded by the favor of God. The forces that are for you are greater than the forces against you.

God has done it for you in the past. He will do it again.

God's got this!

This message was exactly what I needed to keep going. To keep praying. To keep trusting the process. Weeks passed, and Madi continued to get a rose each week. I continued to pray. Protection. Favor. Wisdom. And for God to use Madi in this unlikely journey to bring Him glory.

Hometowns

On October 20, I got a call from a *Bachelor* producer, saying that the bachelor had chosen Madi to be one of the final four and that they would be coming to Auburn for Hometowns. Hmmmm…Final Four. Although I wasn't sure about praying for a "win" in this, I was reminded about praying short! So, I prayed that God would keep Madi in the race as long as He needed to for His glory.

This would be the first time we would see Madi since she left for filming. We were ecstatic—our girl was coming home! We made all the preparations and had everything ready when they arrived. The large camera crew. The producers. The assistants. At 2:00 p.m. we were mic'd up and given instructions for what to expect for the rest of the day.

We sat in the living room anxiously awaiting Madi's arrival. I cannot express the emotions I felt when she walked through that door. We all just joined in one big group hug and cried. Then we all sat down, and she started telling us everything. From the first one-on-one date until the day she came home. It was a lot to take in, but we were so thrilled to have her home that we just listened and cried.

At around 2:00 a.m., we said our goodbyes and watched Madi walk out of our front door again. So many emotions were crowding our minds. I wanted to scream, "Don't go back!" But I knew God wasn't finished with her. The greatest moment and the main reason God allowed her to go on the show were still to come.

The next few weeks seemed like years as we waited.

Over those few weeks, Madi was able to share her faith and take a stand for purity on national television in front of ten million viewers. This was all part of a much bigger picture that we did not understand at the time.

Fast forward to March 9, 2020. The night before *The Bachelor* finale. My husband and I were not invited to the finale, so I flew out to LA to be there when Madi came off the show. I put a letter in her suitcase to encourage her and also to warn her. In the letter I wrote the words, "Madi, someone is going to blindside you. I am not sure who it is, but I know they are, so be ready. Be sure to keep your composure and handle with grace."

As I thought about how to describe what happened at the finale, I decided to share what Madi wrote in her book, *Made for This Moment*.[3] Here is her version of that moment:

> My heart was pounding. I was trembling. There was a knot in my stomach. I'm pretty sure I had already sweat through the hot pink dress I was wearing. And I kept having to go to the restroom. I had no idea what was about to go down. All I knew was that I was about to go on live television with millions of people watching. What would I be asked? How would I respond? I had rehearsed hundreds of times. I was ready. Or was I? I paced. I prayed. I reapplied my lipstick. I prayed some more. I took deep breaths. My heart felt like it was beating out of my chest. The fear of the "what ifs" consumed my mind. What if they

accuse me of something I did not do? What if they set me up? What if the audience cheers against me? Could I do this? I could run away. I could back out. How did I get here?

I had faced so much to get to this moment. I had fallen in love, worked through conflict, taken heat at levels I'd never expected in the public eye about my personal choices, broken up, and now we're on the verge of a second chance.

It was *The Bachelor* finale. The final episode where the Bachelor and his final choice tell the world how they really feel—at the end of the line, after the final rose. It is the only live show of the season. And it is always the most watched.

I was the last girl standing. I should be excited, right?

My producer walks in to tell me that it's time. The soundman attaches my microphone, and I am led backstage. There's no turning back now. I can see the crowd of people in the audience. My heart is beating so hard I thought everyone around me could hear it. I tried to tell myself I had no reason to worry. Surely God led me to this moment. I had prayed about this. Everything leading up to this moment had been so promising. Now all I had to do was walk on that stage, remember what I rehearsed in my mind hundreds of times and speak with confidence. Easy.

And yet, nothing about the next ten minutes was easy. I could have never anticipated what was to come. I walked out on stage and took my seat. The Bachelor, Peter Weber, walked in and sat beside me. Neither of us knew what was about to happen. All we knew was that we wanted this moment to be real, raw, and authentic. This was our moment to be ourselves, to share our feelings, unedited.

The host, Chris Harrison, welcomed us and began asking a series of questions. Everyone in the crowd was silent, just watching and waiting to see what I would say and what I would decide to do. I saw the large camera crew making sure they got every angle and every reaction, from me and from those all around me. As I sat there in that moment, I remembered the words my mother wrote in a letter that she hid in my suitcase the night before the finale. "You are stronger than you realize, Madi. Do not let anything catch you off guard. If anyone blindsides you, respond in love and humility, with confidence." Blindsides you...

Blindside: hit or attack someone on the blind side; attack from an unexpected position

In all of the scenarios I played out in my mind, I never imagined this one. I had imagined being blindsided by the Bachelor. Or one of the girls from the show. Or even one of the producers. I NEVER imagined Peter's mother would be the one to do it, but that's exactly what happened.

I did not understand what was happening in that moment. The first time I met Peter's mother—at her and her husband's vow renewal ceremony— we really hit it off. She loved me and I loved her. It was all so magical. What happened? Something changed. She looked me straight in the eyes and said, "You are not the one for my son. Our family knows it and his friends know it."

My heart skipped a beat. Maybe two. It all happened so fast. She was given so much time to speak. She went on to talk about how I kept the family waiting for hours when they came to meet me later in the season. There was so much I wanted to explain but didn't get the opportunity to. This was not the scenario I had played out in my mind. I felt attacked and misunderstood.

Under most circumstances, my initial response to criticism is to be defensive. To fight back. To retaliate. Somehow, miraculously, I held my tongue. I kept my composure. I felt in that moment, I had to know when to speak and when to be silent. I came in prepared to tell my side of the story. There was so much people didn't see or understand. This was my time to explain everything. For Peter and me to tell the world how we felt about one another and what they didn't get to see from what was aired on the show. But things did not play out as I had planned.

I wish I could put into words what it felt like in that moment. The weight of the words that were being fired at me. The pain of feeling judged, misunderstood, and attacked for my choices and decisions. The heaviness I felt in my chest as I realized that millions were watching. Knowing that my parents were watching. My friends were watching. The world was watching. Words formed in my mouth, but I knew I had to restrain them. I wanted to cry, but knew I had to be strong. I wanted to run off the stage, but I knew I had to stay. I felt I was in a lose-lose. Having only ten minutes on live television, with no pre-produced plan, this was my time to share my heart and let people see all of me, the real, unedited me. It was taken from me. And what could I do? If I cried, I would be seen as weak without a fight in me. If I fought back, I would be seen as angry and disrespectful. All I knew to do was to keep silent and hold my composure as best I could. I tried to form a smile, but even as I did, my lips quivered, knowing tears were soon to follow.

I remember thinking, "Where are you, God?" You led me here. Why did you bring me this far to leave me? Why did you allow me to be set me up like this? Why? In front of millions? I trusted you. I said yes to this journey because you led me here. This is how I get repaid for my obedience?

But God knew what He was doing. He had other plans. Plans I could not understand. Not yet anyway. There was something much bigger going on behind the scenes that I did not understand in that moment.

When I think back to that moment now, I think of the courage it took for me not to retaliate. Courage comes in many forms. Sometimes it's speaking out. Taking a stand. Raising your voice. But sometimes, it's knowing when to remain silent. This was one of those moments. It may have been the most courageous moment of my life. It was definitely the hardest.

As soon as the filming ended, I ran to the back of the studio and broke down. Like a complete breakdown. Peter tried to grab me to stop me from running off. The producers tried to keep me around and get me to talk. But I kept running. Until I found a place to hide and be alone so that I could gather my thoughts. I kept rehashing what just happened in my head and felt so robbed of what should have been my moment to speak my mind and heart. That was my one moment—

no filter, no edit—I was going to get to share it all. It was taken. I felt like a joke, like I was a toy being played with. I was embarrassed, humiliated, and hurt more than I had ever been.

For everyone else this was just entertainment. They watched the finale and then went on with their lives. But for me it was real life. It wasn't just a TV show. It wasn't something I could just turn off and move on.

I had nowhere to go and nobody near me who I felt I could trust or who could understand what I was feeling. No phone. No car. Only the people around me that I felt hurt by.

"You are stronger than you realize, Madi." Those words kept coming back to me. I knew I needed to call my mom. I knew if anyone could help me understand the intensity of what I had just been through, it would be her. As soon as I got my phone back, I called her. She answered and before I could even say a word, she said, "I told you were strong." I began to cry as I felt anything but that. She continued, "Do not waste one second worrying about what just happened. It will serve a greater purpose than you can imagine." Even though I did not understand it all in that moment, I trusted her.

She was right, it did serve a greater purpose. I could have never predicted where my life was going in the next year. Dots were being connected that I could not even see or understand at the time. But God did. He had a bigger purpose in mind. It was in that painful, lonely, and unknown season of life that I discovered the courage I needed to step out and begin."

While this was all happening, I was at the hotel walking the hallway, praying. For three straight hours. The show aired in Central Time, but I wouldn't be able to watch until it re-aired in Pacific Time. While I was pacing and praying, a friend called me. She said, "Tonya, you know what today is? Today is the Day of Purim. Today is the day that Esther went before the king on behalf of the Jews to save a nation." In that moment, I did not fully understand. I hung up the phone, turned my phone off, and went back to praying. This was all leading to something much greater than any of us could have ever imagined.

One of my all-time favorite movies is *Harriet*.[4] If you have not seen it, go see it! I've watched it so many times that I can quote most of the movie. The movie is based on the life of Harriet Tubman, who helped free over 750 slaves. There is a line from the movie where a runaway slave, Minty, makes the statement, "I thought I was going back home to find my husband, but God had other plans for me." As this story unfolds, you will see how Madi thought she was going on *The Bachelor* to find her husband, but God had other, greater plans! God sent Madi to begin a message of purity to lead this generation back to God.

A Global Pandemic

The day after Madi came off of the show, the world shut down. Every news station announced that we were in a global pandemic. Grocery stores were closed. Schools were closed. Businesses were closed. We decided to make the best of the situation, so we went to the beach for the summer. Our family spent more time together during that summer than I can remember in a very long time. And it was much needed! We cooked together, dreamed under the stars, made family TikToks, and cherished every moment.

We managed to stay well for the entire summer. As things started to open back up in the winter, we went back to Auburn and got back into our normal routines.

On December 28, 2020, I was diagnosed with Covid. I could not eat. I could not hold food down, and the thought of food made me sick. I could barely get out of bed. I was so weak that I could only get up to go to the bathroom and get right back in bed. This went on for eight weeks. I lost over fifteen pounds and weighed less than one hundred pounds. I would wake up every day and think it was my last day. I was so sure I wasn't going to live that I wrote goodbye letters to my daughters. I felt so close to death that I started begging God for mercy. I said, "God, please have mercy on me! If You let me live, I will do what You ask me to do." I slowly started eating again. I would go for walks every afternoon. I was gaining my weight back and beginning to live again.

Because the sickness was so bad, I had an extreme fear of going out in public and getting around people. For almost a whole year. I didn't come into contact with people outside of my family. The fear of getting Covid again and coming close to death consumed my mind.

That next October, Madi released her first book. A local bookstore asked her to do a book signing. I could not miss this moment. I rallied every ounce of courage I had and went to that signing. I was so nervous. But I did it.

What I discovered during that season of being so sick was that my suffering was necessary for where God would use me. I was reminded that there are many people who suffer daily, physically and mentally, and who need to know there is hope. I felt that God was saying to me, "You cannot truly preach about the woman with the issue of blood until you've been in a situation where you were desperate to touch the hem of His garment." Sometimes you become the message. Sometimes you have to be willing to invest your own pain. Your own tears. Your own struggles. That sickness is what got me to this day. That sickness is what will propel me to speak more. To write more. To do more for others. I realized that your hardest moments often lead to your greatest moments.

Below are a few points that I wrote in my journal as I reflected back on that time of sickness:

- When you get so tired of the enemy and his attacks, you will do anything. Even if it costs you everything.
- Many times, God will use our deepest pain to propel us into our deepest purpose.
- There may be a cost for going for it, but there's an even greater cost for staying where you are. (In my case, the salvation of many!)

Takeaways:

- God can use an unlikely route to take you where He is leading you.
- Trust God even when it doesn't make sense.
- When God opens a door, trust Him.

CHAPTER 3

Revival

I started living again. My dear friend, Brandy Pearl, and I started leading a college girls' small group. I have to take a second here to tell you there IS NO BETTER group of girls than these girls. And they were vital in what was coming. I remember one particular meeting when we were about to start the lesson, and I stood up and said very boldly, "Something BIG is coming, and you girls will be part of it!" Then I sat back down. Brandy looked at me and whispered, "What's coming?" I just stared at her and said, "I have no idea." One year later, I stood in a circle with those same girls praying for revival on Auburn's campus. That was where it all began.

On January 1, 2023, I sat at the table with my family. It's a tradition for us to write out our "word for the year" along with our goals and dreams and a scripture on New Year's Day. I asked God for five things, and He exceeded my expectations beyond anything I could have imagined. Here's what I wrote:

Word: RISE
Scripture: "Rise up, take courage, and do it" (Ezra 10:4, NIV).

Help start and lead an event.
Speak at an event.
Lead girls to freedom.
Write a book.

The next week, I met with a precious girl who reluctantly shared her story with me of how her life spiraled out of control. She told me how she had grown up in a wonderful Christian family. But after dating the wrong guy for several years, she found herself in the deepest depression imaginable. She would go into her closet and close the door and stay for days. The depression was so bad that she started pulling her hair out and clawing at her skin until she bled. And she would pray that God would not let her live another day because life was too hard to cope.

I met with multiple girls and heard more unimaginable stories. Then one day I sat down with a girl who told me she had been raped on a college campus and that the shame and anxiety she felt caused her to be isolated and to never leave her house. She battled depression and suicidal thoughts and didn't know how she would ever be able to live a normal life again.

That was it. I stood up from that table, and I said, "NO MORE!" I refuse to sit back and watch college students suffer. Not when I serve a God who can heal this generation. So, I called some of my small group girls and said, "We are going to start praying on campus. Praying for God to free students from anxiety, depression, suicidal thoughts, sexual sin, and addiction.

I went to our newly hired football coach...it was his first day on the job! I said, "Coach Freeze, I need permission to get into the football stadium to pray. Our students need prayer." He said, "You have permission, and if anyone gets in your way, call me!"

We met to pray for the first time on Friday, January 20, 2023. As I was walking into the stadium, my oldest daughter, Madison, texted me. She said, "Mom, stop now and read Exodus 33:14–15." I did. Then I shared it with the girls before we entered the stadium. It reads:

"The Lord replied, 'My Presence will go with you, and I will give you rest.' Then Moses said to Him, 'If Your Presence does not go with us, then do not send us up from here.'"

We prayed for one hour that day. Five girls.

I left prayer with the students and received a call from a friend. She asked if I would like to go with her to a women's retreat. I did. The message was on Moses and Exodus 33.

One thing I always tell my daughters is to pay attention when God repeats Himself.

On the third morning, I got up and got dressed to go back to the conference. But God said, "Go back home and go to church with your husband." I didn't understand, but I obeyed. All the way home the enemy kept saying, "The assignment is too big for you. You aren't qualified for what's coming. You can't do this." At this time, I had not had a vision of what was coming.

When I got to church, the pastor stepped up on the stage, and the first thing he said was, "Today's scripture is from Exodus 33:14–15." What he said next really got my attention. He said, "The enemy is telling you that the assignment is too big for you and that you are not qualified for what's coming. But God is going before you and it will happen." What? God is going out of His way to repeat Himself! My heart started racing! I hit my husband and said, "WE ARE GOING TO NEED SECURITY for what's coming!" He patted my leg and assured me it was going to be okay.

The next day, I was on a prayer walk on Auburn's campus when I saw a vision of thousands of students gathered in our basketball arena worshiping together. THE ASSIGNMENT. It was so clear. I started calling campus ministry leaders I had never met and shared the vision. I met with all the local pastors and shared the vision. I met with coaches, administrators, chaplains, and student leaders. I started going into sororities and fraternities. I felt an urgency that I had never felt. And every person I shared it with felt it too.

Every leader that I met with said they were fully in and ready to help. Confirmation that God was going before me.

We had six weeks. So much planning and so much to do to pull off a major production. With the help of ministry leaders, pastors, coaches, and students, we were on our way.

I had been on a recent trip to Waco, Texas, to hear my son-in-law, Grant, interview Pastor Jonathan Pokluda, the lead pastor at Harris Creek Baptist Church. Grant started by saying, "JP, you preached a message at The Porch back in 2015 that changed my life. It was on sexual sin and pornography. I have never been the same since."

My heart started racing. I felt God say, "This is the message JP will speak at Unite."

By the end of that week, I had JP and Passion Music locked in for Unite Auburn. A week later, I was shopping with my daughter, Mallory, when I had an overwhelming feeling that I needed to text Jennie Allen and invite her to speak at the event. After checking her calendar, she said she wouldn't be able to come because she had to be in New York that week. I said, "Well, I understand, but I can't take no for an answer. You are supposed to be there." She said, "Okay. I will be there."

On September 11, 2023, the night before Unite Auburn, I met with a large prayer team to pray for the event. As we were meeting, I felt an overwhelming feeling that God wanted me to speak something: **Unite Auburn, Unite other college campuses, Unite the Nation— it will all be linked to Israel.**

On September 12, 2023, we had Unite Auburn. We didn't sell tickets, and we didn't have registration. We had no idea if 100 or 1000 students would show up. I cannot put into words what I experienced when I walked into the arena and saw over 5000 students gathered. I remember Jennie walking up to me and grabbing my arms, with tears in her eyes, saying, "Tonya, what in the world?" I had no response. Just AWE.

Unite Auburn
    5000 Attended
    200+ Baptisms

The night started with worship by Passion Music, followed by a strong message on sexual sin by Pastor Jonathan Pokluda. Then Jennie Allen spoke on the weight of sin and how to get free. She gave students a moment to confess to one another the thing that kept them bound and from living out their purpose. Students opened up, and there was weeping across the arena. After an altar call where hundreds made a decision for Christ, a student texted one of our local pastors and said, "I need to get baptized tonight!" I told Jennie, "You have to go back on stage. God isn't finished." So Jennie went back on stage and made an announcement that we would be going to a local lake, and everyone was invited to come. Thousands of students RAN a half mile to get to the lake to witness this miraculous moment. One after another, students stepped into the lake, confessing their sins and declaring their need for Jesus. Over two hundred students came forward that night to get baptized. Each student's name was called out as their classmates cheered them on. It was spontaneous and beautiful. A night we will never forget.

One thing that stood out from Unite Auburn was that several pastors contacted me to let me know that their college ministries were in overflow. And fraternity guys that got saved were now leading youth in their church.

Two nights after Unite Auburn, God woke me up at 3:00 a.m. and very clearly said to me, "Form a team. Do it quickly; this will spread fast." I didn't fully understand, but I formed a board, a 501(c)3, and hired three people (with no money, just faith).

The next night, God woke me up at 4:00 a.m. and said, "Mobilize the church." I responded, "I am not a pastor and do not work at a church." He replied, "Mobilize students, and you will mobilize the church."

A week later, God woke me up and said, "Take out your notepad and write this down—this is what you will tell President Trump when you meet him." Again, I didn't understand, but I wrote down what I heard God speak to me. Three weeks later, I was standing in front of President Trump, telling him that revival was going to sweep our nation. It would happen through college students, and he needed to be a part of it.

Testimonies from Unite Auburn:

> "My fraternity brothers and I were baptized together at the event. We confessed years of addiction and our need to be free. After that night, all of us guys got connected with a local church and started serving with high school students."
>
> —Sam

> "I came to the event because a friend invited me. I was considering suicide. I left with the most joy I have ever known. Since then, I have found a church community that holds me accountable and keeps me encouraged in my faith."
>
> —Jeremy

> "My friend invited me to the event. I told her I would not go. Not to church or any Christian event, because I live a life full of sexual

sin, and I do not want a pastor to tell me it's wrong. I ended up going to the event, and of course Pastor JP preached on sexual sin. I felt so condemned and full of shame. After the event, I started to pray and even started going to church. I later realized that it wasn't condemnation or shame but conviction and that I needed to surrender it all to God. I have fully surrendered, and now I help mentor other girls who have battled the same thing. Unite changed my life."

—Michelle

Unite Other College Campuses

After Unite Auburn, we were contacted by many university students begging us to come to their campus. Students reached out on every platform trying to connect with us in hopes of getting Unite on their campus. The same message, but different schools: "We are desperate for God to move on our campus. Our students are lost, hopeless, and even taking their lives. Please come."

As a result, I have had the incredible honor of working with student leadership teams at universities all over the nation. These student leaders are leading prayer on their campus, they are uniting churches and church leaders, they are raising the funding for the events, and they are creating community for students who make a decision to follow Jesus. They are leading us in the greatest revival our nation has ever experienced.

Unite Auburn. Unite other college campuses. It was beginning.

Unite FSU
4,500 Attended
900 Salvations
310 Baptized

Our next stop was Florida State University, the second-largest partying school in the nation. I asked God over and over why He chose FSU for our next stop. The students there did not go to church; they went to bars and parties. They got drunk and went to the campus fountain and dipped in celebration as students turned twenty-one. It seemed so unlikely. But who am I to question God?

Two weeks before the event, I was on a Zoom call with the student team. I realized that no money had been raised and very few students had registered for the event. I asked the team two questions: How are we going to pay for this, and how are we going to get students there? I remember ending the Zoom with a challenge: pray! Pray for God to provide and pray for students to come! And pray we did! And the gifts started pouring in! One after another until the event was fully funded!

We could have never anticipated what would take place at Unite FSU. Close to five thousand students showed up for the event. There were so many incredible stories about that night, but one that stood out to me was that the student team at FSU rented a large bus the day of the event. They had football players and university mascots ride through campus and invite students to jump on the bus and go with them to "a concert." Hundreds of students jumped on the bus, not knowing where they were going.

When the altar call was given, around 900 students came forward. The altar and aisles were filled with students from every direction, forcing through the crowd to get as close to the altar as possible. JP led the students in a prayer of repentance. Then we left the arena to head to the same fountain that students get drunk and celebrate their twenty-first birthday in to witness 310 students get baptized. Including many of those students who jumped on that bus!

The day following the event, the student team of six met to have a "call party." They called all nine hundred students who got saved or baptized! They talked to them about the importance of getting connected to a local church and the importance of community and discipleship. Those calls led to so many students going "all in!"

Testimonies from Unite FSU:

"I confessed something that I never openly confessed to anyone. It was a sin that was holding me back from my relationship with Christ for two years. I feel clean now and ready to begin my relationship with Christ."

—Zach

"I met a group of girls a few months ago outside of a popular club in Tallahassee. I was walking back to my car to drink more, and they were on the corner asking to pray for people. They all prayed for me. I exchanged numbers with one of the girls, and she tried to keep in touch with me. Something always came up, and I was never able to meet with her or join her for church. The months went by, and this morning I texted her asking about going to small group tonight. She told me about Unite, and I found myself here tonight, and I'm more than grateful and joyful to have invited Jesus back into my heart."

—Emma

"I came in today defeated. I am the first in my family attending college. I feel like I'm chosen to break generational curses, but the struggle is real. But today, after worshiping and being in the presence of the Lord, I am CONFIDENT that He can do it. I am going to break this generational curse. The wealth of the Lord starts with me!"

—Genesis

"God set me free from pornography! I'm a Christian, but it was still dominating me. So I gave that up for the first time tonight."

—Jesse

"I finally was able to admit my strongholds to another person out loud. I was so scared, but I did it anyway. I feel like I can finally be free from shame and guilt. I finally understand and can truly trust that Jesus's perfect work on the cross was enough for me. Which means I'm enough, and I don't have to work or prove myself to be good enough for God's love. He loves me and sees me through the rose-colored blood of Jesus. So, I am righteous in God's eyes. I feel happy for the first time in so long. I know life won't be perfect, but I'll be good. I believe that the chains of pornography, weed, insecurity, and perfectionism are falling off. I am free. And it's crazy because none of the things that were said were new to me, but it's like I finally accepted the gift. I finally decided to put my pride and ego and desire to be controlled aside and accept that God's love and grace are sufficient. The verse about confessing your sins to one another so that you can be healed has always haunted me because I knew it was the step I was missing to really experience healing. But after last night, I know it's possible to truly experience healing here and now. I don't have to wait anymore. I have confessed my sins to God and to a friend, and I'm no longer ashamed because there's no condemnation in Christ Jesus. God is good!"

—Miller

Unite Bama
    6,000 Attended
    300 Salvations
    250 Baptisms

The University of Alabama was our next stop. Over 6,000 students packed the arena. The night was filled with incredible worship led by Passion music. Hundreds of students gave their lives to Christ, and over 250 students were baptized in the city fountain.

Alabama is our biggest rival in sports. Our basketball team had advanced in the NCAA tournament and was playing in Spokane, Washington. So was Bama. As we were getting close to the Unite Bama event date, Auburn lost in the tournament, but Bama advanced. So, our family, including my husband (Auburn coach), was all at the Unite event in Bama's basketball arena while Bama was playing in the Sweet Sixteen. As hard as that was, I kept thinking, we are seeing the bigger win here! Salvations, freedom, and baptisms!

Testimonies from Unite Bama:

> "I wanted to let the Unite team know that my Alpha Gam sorority sister attended Unite Bama. It changed her life. She was saved and baptized at the event and decided to go all in with Jesus. Three months after the event, she passed away in a tragic accident. My friend will spend eternity in Heaven because of the decision she made at Unite. Thank you for bringing Unite to Bama. I know hundreds of students made a decision that night."
>
> —Karina

> "I came to Unite so full of unforgiveness and bitterness. My mom passed away when I was seven, and my dad is in prison. I have held resentment towards my dad for as long as I can remember. Something happened during the event. As I confessed what I had held in for

so long, I felt a weight lift off of me. I gave my life fully to Jesus and decided to get baptized. When I stepped into the water, I asked a friend to video record the baptism. I sent a message to my dad. I said, 'Dad, I don't know if you will ever see this, but tonight I choose to forgive you, and I wanted you to see me getting baptized.'"

—Liam

"I am a seventy-year-old mom of four and grandma of twelve who attended Unite Bama with one of my eighteen-year-old twin granddaughters. As an alum, I had to go and see the fruit of my prayers for many years for the University of Alabama campus to break out in spiritual revival, so much so that we will one day see the whole football stadium overflow with ardent worshipers of the Lord Jesus Christ! Thank you for being open and honest to address the issues that so many are challenged with today. During that vulnerable time of confession, my granddaughter and I got very specific and experienced a painful yet precious time of healing, which opened the path to future accountability.

"The time of baptisms was so powerful and sweet! So thankful to be able to experience transformed lives and so honored to continue to pray for each valuable soul to experience the real Jesus, to become more and more like Him, and to flourish in the faith! Praying God's protection and favor on the whole team. May you encounter hearts ripe for receiving the truth of Jesus. May individual lives be transformed to the degree that the faculties and staff, their families, and the culture of each whole college town are changed for His Glory!"

—Sharon

"Unite gave me the opportunity to share my biggest struggles and addictions with another person. It was the first time I'd ever spoken them out loud to someone else. And I got baptized that night in the fountain downtown!"

—Carter

Unite Georgia
8,000 Attended
210 Baptized

Every school was different and had different challenges, but the University of Georgia had unique opposition. It only galvanized our team that God had something GREAT in store there that we couldn't imagine.

One incredibly special thing that we get to do is visit sororities and fraternities before each event. I usually speak to the sororities and let the guys speak to the fraternities. But for Georgia, I had the honor of speaking to the Fiji fraternity.

The entire Fiji fraternity came to the event. Many were saved, and we ended up doing baptisms in truck beds in the Fiji parking lot, where many of the guys were baptized as thousands cheered them on. Following the event, students headed to one of the campus ministries for continued worship until far after midnight.

Testimonies from Unite Georgia:

> "I was an atheist until Christ set me free. And He showed me that the love of Jesus is the greatest love story of all time. Tonight, I decided to go all in with Jesus and was baptized in the back of a pickup truck."
>
> —Antonio

> "I was saved in October and have been waiting for the perfect moment to get baptized. I realized at Unite that there isn't a perfect moment, and there doesn't need to be because I may be imperfect, but He is perfect.

He has helped me fight my anxiety and loneliness and feelings of unbelonging that I've experienced moving out of state for college. It is an ongoing fight and not something that just disappears overnight, but I am committed to picking up my cross daily and choosing Jesus. I have faith that He will deliver on His promises for my life. I know His way is the perfect way, and by surrendering myself to His will, I will be led in the right direction. Thanks to Unite, I've learned to fully embrace my imperfection and lean on His perfection to guide my life."

—Suri

"My sister and I traveled from Maryland to attend the Unite event. I'm so blessed to have been a part of this! God is moving in Georgia, and I felt His spirit before worship even began! What an incredible experience to witness chains being broken and people's lives changed! I have been blessed just by being there, and the spontaneous baptisms made my heart so happy! I celebrated with every single person without even knowing them! What a blessing! Thank you, Georgia, for welcoming me, and Unite, thank you for following God's lead and being obedient!"

—Daniela

"Last night was one of the most amazing nights of my life. The faith in that room was echoing off the walls. I attended with a majority of the Cheer team from the University of West Georgia, and I truly believe that our program and the people within will forever be changed after last night. FIVE OF MY TEAMMATES GAVE THEIR LIVES TO JESUS CHRIST LAST NIGHT! I am so beyond grateful I was able to experience their choices and watch them dedicate themselves to the Lord. GOD WAS IN THE ROOM!"

—Logan

"I've been hiding my sin away from God and everyone else in my life. I've struggled with pornography since I was eleven years old. I used it to cope with life. I was living in anxiety and fear that I felt I've never wanted to say out loud because I was ashamed; I didn't want God to know. But He knows. When we were all confessing last night, I went with the basic answer: alcohol. In reality, what I needed and wanted to confess was that I was using these things in a way that was not honoring to God. God knew how much I was struggling with that. My friend also came last night and gave her life to Jesus. It was her strength to also talk about struggling with the same sin that pushed me to tell her about my own struggles. I truly believe that God used her to show me there is no condemnation for those who are in Christ Jesus. UNITE changed my life last night. I experienced His presence in a whole new way that I never thought imaginable. I give all the glory to God for how my life has been changed."

—Graham

"Up until last night I was hiding, and I felt stuck. I was so shameful and believed I was unworthy of being in the Lord's presence. After last night, I feel free again, and I want to go to Him every single day."

—Penny

Unite Tennessee
  7,000 Attended
  200 Baptized

Our fifth campus was the University of Tennessee. Students flew in from Maui, Hawaii, and drove from

Massachusetts, New Jersey, New York, Alabama, Indiana, and many other states to witness what God was doing on college campuses. Hundreds dedicated their lives to Christ, and hundreds were baptized. Students testified to experiencing freedom from years of addiction, depression, and suicidal thoughts. Many have shared since the event that they have reconciled broken relationships, started serving in their local church, and many have walked away from unhealthy relationships.

Fox News did special coverage of the event, interviewing students the night of and the morning after. The testimonies were powerful!

Testimonies from Unite Tennessee:

> "My sister gave her life to Jesus and got baptized at Unite Tennessee. I get to spend eternity with my sister."
>
> —Hailey

> "I grew up in a Christian household, had the best family and support system possible, and did all of the things that religion told me that I needed to do to be a Christian. I got saved and baptized at a really young age (so young that I don't even remember it at all), and as I got older, I never fully understood the concept of a relationship with God, but I still believed in Him.

"Last summer I went through the hardest time of my life. I had just graduated high school, and I was in the biggest battle of spiritual warfare that I had ever faced. I was facing some health issues that caused me to spiral into an anxious mess. Also, the enemy was using some past trauma to eat away at my soul and heart until I just went numb. I didn't know if I believed in God. My fiancé (now husband) looked at me at one point and told me that I was just a shell of myself. It was like I was physically on earth but not living. I was quiet. I was hurting. I couldn't go one day without at least four anxiety attacks that left me numb and lifeless. The enemy had me so convinced that my problems would not be solved unless I was just not alive. I had fully given up, and I didn't know what else to do except give it to God.

"From that point on, which was October 2023, I have been working on fully surrendering to God. But I have still struggled with finding commitment and a relationship with Him. I felt as though I was living a double life. I was preaching about what Jesus had brought me out of, but I wasn't spending alone time with Him. I would give my friends advice on how to handle their hardships, but just five months earlier, I was in the deepest pits of my life and lifeless. I felt like a fraud, and I felt unqualified.

"So I came into last night with an open mind. I had no idea what it was about. I didn't know who was speaking or singing. I just saw an Instagram post about it on someone's story, and I felt like I needed to be there. So I simply just showed up. My eyes were opened beyond my imagination. I realized that I was carrying around so much weight from my past. I wasn't fully opening up myself to God, and I saw that He is so ready for a relationship with me. The things that are holding me back from a relationship with Him are lies from Satan. I am qualified to share my story. I do not have to be a fraud. Even though I was in the deepest pits of my life just five months ago, God has loved me through it all and has wanted a relationship with me all along.

"And so last night I made a commitment to God and myself that I was going to acknowledge that He has always been there and that my shame has kept me from a relationship with Him. It made me realize that I was being prideful by thinking that my shame was too big for God. So, I begged God to tear down the walls of pride and shame and allow Him to dwell in me. I also didn't know that there would be baptisms after the event, but it felt like the best possible thing to do to solidify my commitment with God and publicly announce that I am different from here on out. My chains of shame are gone, and now I can live in the freedom of having a deep relationship with Jesus Christ, who saved me for that reason! The old has passed away, and He is making all things new in my life.

"I couldn't be more grateful for coming to an event that I knew nothing about. Last night radically changed my life. And I now fully know Jesus as my Lord and Savior!"

—Fraida

"In my personal life, I struggle with sin constantly. I have a deep fear of man. I struggle with intense anxiety, and I lose the fight against temptation on a daily basis. My actions revolve around what people will think of me rather than what the Lord is asking me to do. I try desperately to hide my sin in order to keep up my image as a 'good Christian girl.' Unite showed me that I am not alone. To see so many of my peers step out in boldness and admit to struggling with the same sins was so powerful. Satan had been isolating me, making me believe that I was the only Christian struggling with these things and that my faith was invalid because of it. I was doubting my salvation.

"When I confessed my sin out loud at UNITE, I felt that stronghold of isolation being broken. I am no longer walking alone. I am broken, and I am sinful. But the Lord's blood is enough, and who am I to tell Him that it's not? He has blessed me with a community to walk alongside me as I seek to turn away from my sin. Satan had blinded me to that blessing, telling me that I would be rejected and outcast if they knew what I struggled with. Satan's lies no longer have a place in my mind. I am a child of God, and the truth of His Word reigns triumphant over Satan's deception. Thank you, UNITE, for changing my life!"

—Heather

"I came with a group of eight from Purdue University! We drove six and a half hours to Knoxville, and it was so worth it. I have no words for what God did last night, and it inspired us all so much to keep praying for God to MOVE at Purdue! We are all super passionate about unity ministry on our campus, so hearing the stories of students who have been with Unite since Auburn and listening to how it all started was incredible. I truly believe God is reviving this generation by waking up college campuses across the nation, and we want to be a part of it! Lives are being changed, people are being set free, and sparks are being lit that I pray will be fanned into flames to reach more and more people for Christ! Jesus is King, and I want everybody to know it!"

—Bryson

"For months I have felt incredible shame from sexual impurity in past relationships. I had asked God to forgive me and restore me, and even though I believed that He had forgiven me, I still felt the weight and burden of shame. Last night, the burden was lifted, and I now feel FREE of the shame and fully redeemed and restored and forgiven! Glory to God, He is SO good! Thank YOU for bringing revival to our campus, city, and state—we needed this, and it was SO apparent how God moved!"

—Harper

"Hi! Unite honestly changed my life last night. I wasn't even going to go because I had to work, but I really felt the Lord calling me to go, so I gave up my shift and went. Before last night, my boyfriend and I had really been struggling with sexual impurity. To put it plainly, we really struggle with not having sex. The night before Unite, we had a conversation like, okay, how do we do this? We really need to fix it; we just desperately don't know how or who to talk to about it.

"He was sitting with his friends, and I was sitting with mine, and although we were separate, we knew we both needed to hear Jennie's message. We later found out that we both said during the two minutes Jennie gave during her message to confess a sin that we struggled with sexual impurity. After both messages, we were worshiping, both super convicted about what we knew we needed to do. So, he came over to me during the message and started praying for the Lord to change our hearts and give us the strength to do it the right way.

"We both made the decision last night that we were going to do things the right way so that our marriage will flourish one day. Personally, I've heard Jennie's message before at Passion a few years ago. That message is what changed my life. The last time I heard that message, I confessed my sin of thoughts of suicide. Hearing it again was honestly just a reminder to me of how good our God is and how He changes everything.

"I now am about to go into ministry. I know it's not Jennie that saved my life, it's Jesus, but I'm so thankful for Jennie's genuineness and truth that the Lord uses to speak through her. Thanks to that message, my boyfriend and I have chosen to take the necessary steps to have a God-honoring relationship by being pure, and I believe that will change our lives forever. I knew last night would be good, but I had no idea it would be THAT good. Thank you for a great night and for doing everything behind the scenes, paying to have everything you did, praying over our campus and the people coming, practicing, and just making it happen. I love to see what you guys are doing for every campus you're going to. Thank you, thank you, thank you!"

—Melinda

"Last night during the no condemnation, my friend and I began to share with each other.

Once we finished and hugged it out, we saw this guy in front of us not talking to anyone. We introduced ourselves, and we found out his name was Preston. We shared what was heavy on our hearts, and I felt God calling me to ask if I could pray for him. After we prayed, we listened to the talk more, and after JP said if we wanted to come up during the prayer, we could. My friend Preston and I went up and prayed, and then we worshiped Jesus. After, the team talked about baptism, and Preston decided to get baptized. I didn't know his story, and as he was getting baptized, he told everyone that he had just moved here and had been so alone. But in there he was free and not alone. God is so good."

—Tesa

Unite South Carolina
4,500 Attended
150 Baptized

Unite South Carolina reminded me a lot of how it felt going into FSU. It was the first school of the semester and a struggle to get momentum with the logistics and with fundraising. We were questioning if we should even go—was God moving there—what was happening? But God showed up. Thousands of students showed up to experience the freedom of Jesus. Thousands of students ran to the altar and fell to the floor in repentance before an altar call was even given!

Testimonies from Unite South Carolina:

"There's never a 'good' time to lose someone we love so much, but we have had a chance, over the past week, to really see the impact he made on his family, friends, and community, and we are just so grateful and inspired as we have gotten a glimpse at how special he was to so many people. We're especially grateful to the Lord for some really impactful times over even just the last few weeks, where our daddy was greatly moved by a presentation of the Gospel at a Colonial Life Arena event (@unite_us) and shared it with us and many others. How incredibly awesome of the Lord to use that place that he loved so much (@CLA) to minister to his soul in a special way in his last week of life."

—Carla

"I decided last minute to come to the event. I came in with so much heaviness and hopelessness. My fiancé has battled pornography for many years, and it has caused so much stress in our relationship. I broke up with him the day before the event and just felt like I couldn't cope anymore. I considered taking my life. At the event, one of the leaders prayed for me, and I felt so much peace. I know that I will move forward from this, and God will redeem it all. Unite saved my life."

—Aimee

"Just a little of my story... God has been so good to me. Just this year alone, I went through a lot, from sleeping in my car to losing jobs because of depression and anxiety taking control. I went to Unite South Carolina 2024. It was great, and I enjoyed it, but what stuck was when Jennie Allen gave the illustration of the devil wanting us to remain hidden and stuck behind the shame and guilt of doing things we know aren't right but can't seem to let go.

"Before that night, July 17 was supposed to be my last day in this world. I tried hard to take myself out. But God had other plans. I took a bottle of 270 sleeping pills and 6 oz of liquid sleeping medicine. I cut deep into the flesh in my neck, arms, and legs. And that night when I got pulled over by a cop, he found me bleeding over everything. I had ignored everyone and went contactless with the world because I was done with life. I got sent to the hospital and was there overnight. My parents came and got me the next day and brought me home.

"For weeks I wanted to do nothing, but fast forward—I found a counselor to help me process my feelings, and I have been growing in God more and more each day. God is not done with my story; it was time for me to let go of the pen and let Him take over. Every day is a blessing to be alive, to bask in the glory of God and thank Him for new life and a new perspective on life to help draw others to experience the goodness of God!"

—Wyatt

Unite Arkansas
10,000 Attended
200 Baptized

Unite Arkansas felt incredible from the beginning. With a student leadership team that was so passionate and FIRED UP, we knew it would be a standout event. They believed and had faith for SO many students to show up and pack the arena. And the students showed up. We had more students pre-register than ever before, and over ten thousand attended that night.

There was a moment at the end of the night when the spirit of God was so strong that the students were on their knees and the worship continued for hours. No one wanted to leave. The presence of the Lord was so evident. I truly believe miracles happened in that room that we may never know about.

Testimonies from Unite Arkansas:

> "I stayed until nearly 1 am worshiping out on the lawn. It stirred my heart for the Lord. I got a ride back to my car from a guy who hosts a Bible study in town, and he invited me to it. Didn't think much of it until over a month later when a friend of mine invited me to the same exact group of 20–30 people. I saw this as a sign that the Lord wanted me to be in fellowship with these people, and it has already helped to strengthen my faith. Praise the Lord!"
>
> —Isaac

> "I'm a sophomore and a new transfer student. When I arrived here, I envisioned living the college dream. During my first week on campus, I received a blue flyer from a college min-

istry called C3, which announced a free concert featuring Christian singers. I had never been to a concert before, so I decided to go. To make a long and wonderful story short, the speaker at the event was phenomenal. A blonde lady began asking questions that I was too afraid to even think about, let alone answer out loud. It felt as though someone understood me, and the atmosphere seemed safe enough for me to confront my fears of rejection. I had never experienced someone truly understanding me before. When she mentioned that there is someone greater than herself who understands us and died for our sake, I found myself eager to learn more. That night, I was able to share what had been on my heart for too long, and I was set free and baptized. Just thinking about that night and the sense of community fills me with happiness every time."

—Lindsay

"It brought to light a fire in my friend group that eventually led us to start a small group together. I saw another friend get baptized and another friend experience the joy of Christ for the first time!"

—Della

"My friend and I were able to confide in each other, and we both found FREEDOM FOR THE FIRST TIME! We told each other things we've never told anyone, and we are lighter because of it and because of the grace of God!"

—Mateo

"Hi! I walked in last night with a lot of shame and sin weighing heavy. On the way there, I was praying, asking GOD for forgiveness for my sins of the night before, and struggling to believe He would actually forgive them. I genuinely thought to myself, 'Eventually, His forgiveness must run out. He must be getting tired of me continually messing up.' And I thought, 'I wish I knew more verses about forgiveness. I know the Bible says there's no condemnation for those in CHRIST, but how can that be true? That can't be right because I feel so much shame.'

"I am someone who is usually very secure in my faith and relationship with Jesus! So, when JP asked, 'How sure are you that you'll go to heaven?' I immediately thought, 'Obviously ten because Jesus Christ died for me, and He's the only way to heaven!' But as we started raising our hands, I felt such overwhelming doubt creep in. As I look back on it, I truly feel it was the enemy who whispered to me, 'Can you really be that sure? You really think YOU can be 100 percent positive you're going to heaven? Think of what you did just last night. Surely, you'll do something to mess it up.' So many thoughts like this took over my mind. I've never felt such intense doubt as this. So, I raised my hand when he said 'nine.'

"Nearing the end of his sermon, I knew I had been wrong. He had us stand up if we said any number other than ten. And then he said something that I truly needed to hear. 'How arrogant of you to assume something you do could get you in or out.' Ouch. But how true! I was reminded that my sin does not disqualify me from the FATHER! That's WHY He sent the SON to die for my sins!

"I also felt GOD reveal to me that I had been giving the enemy a foothold when I sin! And that's how those doubts were able to creep in—those LIES that discounted me from my INHERITANCE as a child of GOD! This was a much-needed reminder that there is NO condemnation for those in CHRIST JESUS! GOD truly answered my prayers from before and spoke DIRECTLY to what I was feeling.

What a blessing that He listens and meets me where I am!"

—Robert

Unite Mississippi State
  6,000 Attended
  150 Baptized

We felt from the very beginning of the Mississippi State event that there would be something special that night for our team. Circuit Rider music joined us for the event—it was really powerful for our team. They prayed over us, and we felt God moving in our pre-service huddle. There is something so special about spirit-filled worship with friends. The pre-service gathering set the stage for an even more powerful night with students.

Testimonies from Unite Mississippi State:

"I repented of a sin I had not been 100 percent sure was a sin. Unite helped me solidify the fact that it was, and ever since then, I have left it behind. I believe in Romans 8:1. It has helped me see the Lord and His goodness. It made me realize how much I needed Him, and since then, December 5 will mark sixty-six days of consistently reading the Word of God and praying to Him daily. Sixty-six days is what it takes to make a habit that sticks for a lifetime, and I am proud to say it started October 1, right after the Unite event! God is good, and Unite helped me see that good God I had known for years and actually appreciate Him and include Him in my life!"

—Wesley

"I attended the MSU Unite event, and my boyfriend attended the Ole Miss Unite event. It began to raise conversations about our faith and how the physical part of our relationship was not glorifying God. The conversations were difficult, but we are in such a better place now because of it. We were able to commit that area of our relationship to the Lord when we had been holding it to ourselves. Watching others be so open about their sin struggles allowed us to be open about our own. Thank you so much!"

—May

"Hi! Last night was the best night ever. From the moment the speakers began to speak, it felt like they were talking right to me. I grew up going to church and believing in God. I thought I was saved back in 2021, but for some reason, I always had this doubt that my sin was keeping me from going to heaven. When Jonathan asked us to 'raise your hands if you think you're 1–9 on getting to heaven,' I raised my hand at nine, but I didn't want to feel like that anymore. I didn't want to doubt that I was getting into heaven because I love Jesus, and I'm so thankful for what He did for me and for rising from the dead. But when we prayed that prayer out loud and unashamed, then afterward, I did not have that fear that I'm not going to get into heaven. I completely and fully trust God with everything in me and my soul. That doubt I had is gone. When we went outside to be baptized, my heart has never been filled with so much joy as it was with that decision. Thank you all for coming to Tennessee. So many souls were saved, and I'm happy to say that mine was one of them."

—Aiden

Unite Ole Miss

    7,000 Attended

    1,000+ Salvations

    120 Baptized

I have to say, Unite Ole Miss was an unforgettable one. It was the first of three where over a thousand students came forward for salvation. The baptisms following the event went far past 1:00 a.m. God moved like never before!

Testimonies from Unite Ole Miss:

"September 27, 1971, I invited Christ to come into my life on the Ole Miss campus. After graduation, I ventured into ministry and have served for almost forty-nine years. I believed Christ was coming back any day; therefore, I did not go to seminary. I needed to share my faith. I lived with a heart of helping to fulfill the Great Commission. I live in Little Rock and arrived early for Unite on the Rebel Campus. I sat up high in the arena and prayed; that was why I came. I prayed for every student who attended, and I drove the campus the next day praying for students and faculty. I was amazed by how many students walked in with their Bible, pen, and paper. Then, to see so many come forward. Light speed from 1971 to now—if the students would really understand how fast this life goes. Thanks for your work. I will continue to pray!"

—James

"God changed my life at UNITE! I am from Auburn, Alabama, and never got to attend

UNITE because I was always so caught up in my sports and idolized everything else in the world over Jesus. Getting baptized was heavy on my heart for the past month, and then I heard that UNITE was coming to Ole Miss. I was feeling a pull to get baptized and publicly declare how the Lord removed shackles from my life that I never thought I would lose. So I was blessed to have the privilege of getting baptized in a truck bed and testify to the love of our God!"

—Ian

"This night was just absolutely amazing! It lifted me up in so many ways, and I don't think I had ever been around that many Christians in a single area. It was all inspiring and honestly filled the room with so much joy and laughter!"

—Maya

"Unite was really the first step I took in reigniting my relationship with God. I was saved in the fourth grade but was unaware of what it fully meant to be a follower of Christ. I began living for the world throughout high school but knew it wasn't what God had in store for me. Unite taught me that God is so eager for a relationship with us, and he welcomes us with open arms no matter what we bring to Him. It was very eye-opening and reassuring to know that I hadn't messed up to the point of damaging our relationship. From there, I knew I wanted to be baptized! I've had so many God moments in the weeks since unite, and it has been so amazing. Our relationship has never been stronger, and I've never been happier!"

—Jamie

Unite Florida
6,000 Attended
1,000+ Salvations
175 Baptized

The night before Unite Florida, students from eight different universities gathered for hours of prayer and worship. Prayer precedes a move of God. And that's exactly what we saw! God moved at the University of Florida! More than a thousand students accepted Jesus as their Lord and Savior, and hundreds were baptized.

Testimonies from Unite Florida:

"I recently attended Unite at the University of Florida and Gainesville! It was an absolutely amazing experience and completely transformed my life. I recently gave my life to Christ a few years ago, and it was the best decision I've made, but I've always been looking for opportunities to try to get closer to the Lord and engage in more Christian-based activities! I recently made some new Christian friends within the past few months, and they were kind enough to invite me to the event. I was one of the many people who were called to the front to praise and worship, and just being so close and being able to experience something so real and amazing brought tears to my eyes! And it made me realize how much I love the Lord and helps me realize that everything I have is because of him. I think it is a beautiful thing that the Lord is pushing and moving people to do things like Unite!"

—Tabitha

"I am a twenty-one-year-old girl, and I have been single my entire life. Not only have I just been single, I've never been approached by a man, nor has a man ever shown an interest in me. I deeply desire to be a wife and mother, so my never-changing relationship status has really brought me down for quite some time.

It sounds silly, but I worry every day about never getting married. I pray for my future husband every day, and I talk to God about my worries about this a lot.

"I will never forget what happened to me at Unite Tennessee. I heard God speak to me for the first time ever. Jennie Allen had everyone close their eyes and imagine themselves at their favorite spot. I pictured myself at my favorite fishing/sunset watching spot, which is where I feel God's presence the most. She then asked us to imagine Jesus sitting next to us at our favorite spot. She told us to tell God whatever we had on our hearts and in our minds, then she asked what He was doing/saying. In that moment, I asked God where my husband is and if I'll ever have one. I immediately heard Jesus say, 'It will happen,' and I felt immense peace and a weight lifted from my shoulders. I knew it was God speaking to me, and my eyes immediately started tearing up—I started to cry. I had never heard God's voice before, but I knew it was Him when I felt His presence as He spoke to me. That moment has brought me so much clarity and peace. I know now that God has a husband in store for me, but it will still take a lot of faith to get to that point in my life whenever the time is right."

—Molly

Unite Texas A&M
10,000 Attended
1,050 Salvations
250 Baptized

It was the most amazing ending to our fall semester! Students from thirty-six different universities joined the students of Texas A&M for an incredible night of worship. All day leading up to the event, I kept feeling like God was saying, "Call students to their purpose!" As the event was coming to a close, I questioned if I really heard God. Then Jennie walked up to me and said, "Tonya, we have to call students to their purpose!" I knew then that God was confirming what He had already told me. Jennie and I went back on stage and finished the night with a challenge to students to discover and live out their purpose.

Again, over one thousand students came forward for salvation, and hundreds were baptized.

Testimonies from Unite Texas A&M:

"When going to UNITE, I had no expectations. I obviously saw the event online but never understood all the life change that was going to happen. As Jennie Allen was speaking, I felt a tug in my heart about what I had been praying about, which was what my calling is and how I should go about my calling. Jennie made it very clear that it is important to serve His kingdom wholeheartedly and very important to also have community to help you when life gets hard.

"As we prayed after her message and talked to others about my struggles and what I've been praying about, the Lord just allowed me to confess what my thoughts had been consumed by—my calling. JP then went up and talked about how thinking too much about myself will keep me from going all in. Tying this to what Jennie said, it's not about what I want for my life but how I can better serve Him. With lots of prayer afterward, I realized that the only way is to surrender that to Him. I got an overwhelming peace over my next steps and have never felt better!"

—Alex

"Jennie Allen led us through a confession activity, where I realized I had never truly confessed to Jesus the things of my past. I was trying to live for Him while still holding on to certain worldly things I realized I had never let go of. Jonathan used the analogy of a baboon holding onto something while trying to get its hand out of the box. This was me! That night, I rededicated my life to Jesus Christ, giving my FULL self to Him and not looking back. I'm so thankful for His never-ending love and mercy and how Unite reminded me of that."

—Ezra

"I've been struggling with mental health all semester and simply not choosing to believe God actually cares for and loves me. Right in the middle of the speaker's session, when we were talking about no condemnation, a random girl came to me, offered to pray over me, and spoke into the private fears, thoughts, and lies from the enemy that had been constantly in my head that I had told nobody about. She prayed over them, and I felt God's peace in my heart. I have felt it since."

—Tara

"The Lord met me at Unite and smiled at me while I confessed my deepest sin. He showed me that there is mercy and grace in abundance for ALL believers, not only new believers."

—Dakota

Unite Kentucky
   8,000 Attended
   2,000 Salvations
   200 Baptized

Unite Kentucky will always be special to me because it was the first event that I spoke at. I shared the incredible story of the last five years that I am sharing in this book. After the event, I heard one testimony after another from students who said for the first time they believed in God. It was truly a night of miracles.

Leading up to Unite Kentucky, the local student team met weekly to pray and even had Jericho marches, with students circling campus and walking as many as forty miles in continuous prayer. These prayer gatherings are the reason two thousand students came forward to receive Christ and are now going all in and getting connected with local churches.

Testimonies from Unite Kentucky:

> "After hearing Tonya's message tonight, I believe in God now."
>
> —Tyler

> "I lost my father at the ripe age of seventeen, and I turned away from God and blamed Him for it all for the longest time. And now, two and a half years later, I am returning back to

Him. You forgave your father, but I forgave our Father in heaven after always blaming him for taking my dad away as a senior in high school."

—Sean

"I attended Unite last night. I want to express my gratitude for sharing your story about your father. It resonated deeply with me, as it mirrors my own experience. My father was emotionally abusive, an alcoholic, and instilled fear in me during my childhood. Now, as an adult, I have ended my relationship with him, yet I still harbor feelings of hatred. Your words, 'It takes two to reconcile, but only one to forgive,' impacted me. I have often prayed for God to mend our relationship, but these feelings have only led to anger and sadness. Recognizing that as Christians, we are called to forgive others since God forgives us, I have already noticed changes in my heart. Thank you for providing this perspective for me and thank you again for sharing your story."

—Ebony

"Thank you so much for the message last night. I have found God again."

—Roan

Unite Ohio State
7,000 Attended
2,000+ Salvations
150 Baptized

Let me take you back to how Unite Ohio State even came to be. I got a DM from one of the girls on Ohio State's dance team. She said, "Mrs. Tonya, I beg you to come to Ohio. We are ripe for revival." She had my attention. I told her to find other students to help lead locally. On the first Zoom call, one of the students made a comment that seemed really bold but also prophetic. He told me with confidence that their football team would win the National Championship, and then Unite Ohio State would follow. Not only did the football team win the National Championship but the dance team did too! And Unite followed.

There was heavy snow and freezing temperatures leading up to the event. That did not stop seven thousand students from showing up to get in the presence of the Lord. Following the event, students lined up outside in nine-degree temperatures to be baptized in heated U-Haul trucks. God is moving and nothing can stop Him!

Testimonies from Unite Ohio State:

> "My boyfriend passed away after a long battle with cancer. I was so lost after that, but to-

night I promised to never question God again and make it my mission to share our story and bring more people to Christ. I came to Unite with some friends, and their lives were changed. I am lining up cars to bring as many as I can to Purdue because I know more people need what I experienced."

—Sadie

"I attended Unite last night and just wanted to say how inspiring your story was. I gave my life to Christ in November of 2023 after being a 'sugar baby' (having sex for money and gifts) and having an abortion in October of 2022. The moment I walked into Planned Parenthood, my choices were taken away from me. The only option I was presented with was the type of abortion I wanted. No one mentioned adoption or even considered telling me I'd be a great mother. It wasn't until I got home after taking the abortion pill and saw my lifeless child in my hands... that recognition was true evil... it rocked my world.

"Since coming to Christ, I've felt a conviction on my life to start a pro-life clinic that will eventually defund and replace Planned Parenthood. I have no idea how I will do this. I have no idea where to start. I am not qualified. I am not smart enough. And I barely have enough resources to pay my rent every month. But YOUR story gave me HOPE."

—Rose

"Your testimony literally changed my life. My parents have been divorced, and I have little to no contact with my father. After your testimony, I called my father and told him I forgive him for everything. Since that day, my father has called every single day to check on me. I found freedom from years of unforgiveness and get to spend the rest of my life in a relationship with my dad."

—Calvin

Unite Purdue

4,500 Attended

500+ Salvations

100 Baptized

Unite Purdue was unique and incredibly powerful. It was unique in that it was the only event that was held in the university's music hall and not the basketball arena. It was incredibly powerful, as worship lasted for hours beyond the time the event typically ends. God's presence was so strong that the students did not want to leave.

Testimonies from Unite Purdue:

"I came to the event feeling numb. Feeling unseen, overlooked, and questioning my purpose. I felt God speak to me and remind me why I am here and that He has chosen me for something big. I must obey, even when it does not make sense. Unite changed my life."
—Sashi

"The worship was incredible. I did not want it to end. I would have stayed in the room all night. Thank you for bringing Unite to Purdue."
—Ava

Unite West Virginia
5,000 Attended
1,000+ Salvations
120 Baptized

Unite West Virginia was covered in prayer. Students met weekly, walking up to forty-nine miles, praying for God to move on their campus. And God heard their prayers. From the first song to the last song, students were deeply engaged in worship and prayer.

Testimonies from Unite West Virginia:

"I served on the local student team. I was so afraid students would not come to the event. We had many students say they did not want to attend a religious event, and they didn't want Jesus mentioned on campus. But we prayed. For months, we prayed. And there was not an empty seat in the arena. God heard our prayers and lives were changed for eternity."

—Jayden

"I was blown away by the amazing worship by *Elevation Rhythm!* The speakers were incredible, and the testimonies during baptisms blessed me in ways I could have never expected. I love what God is doing through this movement. West Virginia will never be the same!"

—Marcus

Unite SMU

3,500 Attended
300 Salvations
100 Baptisms

SMU was a smaller, more intimate gathering of students. Kari Jobe and Cody Carnes, along with Tiffany

Hudson, led powerful worship. After Jennie and JP's message, students lined up to confess sins and addictions and left it all at the altar. It was a night of freedom.

Testimonies from SMU:

> "I was part of the local student team that helped plan and promote the event. I grew closer to Jesus from serving on the team. The experience was unlike anything I have ever been a part of. Getting to help lead a movement like Unite on my campus was one of the greatest blessings of my life."
>
> —Jay

> "My little brother gave his life to Jesus and got baptized at Unite SMU. I walked into his bedroom the next day, and he was listening to Christian music. I have never heard my brother play Christian music. I will forever be thankful for the difference Unite is making in the lives of my generation."
>
> —Amari

Unite Baylor
   5,000 Attended
   230 Salvations
   70+ Baptisms

As I prayed about Unite Baylor, I knew God was saying this one would be different. The message needed to be more focused on purpose. I shared the incredible story of Unite and all that God has done since 2023. Then I challenged students to not waste one day of their lives and to be obedient in what God was calling them to do.

At the end of the night, hundreds of students surrendered to God's calling on their lives. Many of those students testified that God was leading them to missions. I can only imagine the ripple effect of that night.

Testimonies from Unite Baylor:

> "I have been an atheist my whole life. I was studying at the common grounds and saw a big crowd of people walking. I decided to follow them and ended up at the basketball arena where Unite was happening. I surrendered my life to Jesus a few hours later."
>
> —Jorge

> "Last night I decided to go all in with Jesus and surrender to a call on my life. I know God is telling me to start going to church, and I will obey."
>
> —Avery

"I have been studying law at Baylor. Tonight, God has called me to be a missionary to the nations. My life will never be the same."

Looking Ahead: More to come for Unite 2025

During huddle at each of our events, we always thank God for what He did at the previous events. We all say together, "Thank You, God, for what You did at Auburn. Thank You for what You did at FSU. Thank You for what You did at Bama. Thank You for what You did at Georgia. Thank You for what You did at Tennessee. Thank You for what You did at South Carolina. Thank You for what You did at Arkansas. Thank You for what You did at Mississippi State. Thank You for what You did at Ole Miss. Thank You for what You did at Florida. Thank You for what You did at Texas A&M. Thank You for what You did at Kentucky. Thank You for what You did at Ohio State. Thank You for what You did at Purdue. Thank You for what You did at West Virginia. Thank You for what You did at SMU. Thank you for what you did at Baylor."

Then we all ask God to do it again!

We are believing for bigger things to come as we continue to visit campuses in the fall of 2025. We are already slated to visit six more universities.

I am so expectant and cannot wait to see God do it again! SOMETHING ABOUT NOT PRAYING SHORT—

Even with all we've witnessed, we refuse to pray short and are believing God to do far beyond what we've seen or could imagine!

Takeaways:
- Prayer precedes a move of God.
- There is no greater investment than investing in others.
- Your pain can always lead to purpose.
- NOTHING is impossible with God.

CHAPTER 4

Learn to Forgive So You Fulfill Your Destiny

One thing that I learned on the journey of the last five years of my life is that the enemy will use your past, your pain, and your present to try to keep you from walking fully in your purpose. You will have to find ways to deal with those things that keep you bound, distracted, and isolated so that you can discover your true destiny and live it out.

I want to share a story with you about a girl and her father:

Most little girls wish for a puppy, a new baby doll, or a beautiful necklace, but I always wished for a dad. My dad wasn't there the day I was born. He wasn't there when I started kindergarten. He wasn't there to teach me how to ride a bike. He wasn't there to hug me when I had a bad day or to cheer for me when I played sports.

He wasn't there for my high school graduation, and he was not there to walk me down the aisle on my wedding day. I remember watching other girls with their dads growing up, wishing just once I had a dad to run to after school, to dance with at the daddy-daughter dance, to teach me to throw the ball in the yard, or to tell me I was beautiful in my prom dress.

I never told anyone how desperately I longed for a father. I just kept it buried deep inside. Over time, I grew to resent my father for not being there in the moments I needed him. But the thing that angered me most was the way he treated my mother. He battled with alcoholism and had multiple affairs. He would show up at our house, often drunk, begging for my mother to take him back. She would give him chance after chance. And every time he would end up physically and mentally abusing her, right in front of us kids. Then he would leave again. Leaving my mother more broken than she was before.

My mother worked several jobs to be able to provide for four children. She did everything she could to make sure we had food and a roof over our heads. But with no help from my father, it wasn't always enough. There were times we did not have any food in the house or money to go buy any, so we would go outside and gather pecans or berries just to have something to eat. Sometimes my mother couldn't afford to pay the electric bill, so we would have to load up in the car and drive to my grandmother's until payday. I cannot imagine the shot to my mother's pride. The worst memory I have was when I made cheerleader for the first time, and I had to see the look on my mother's face when she had to tell me that I would not be able to cheer at the first game because she did not have the money to buy the required cheer shoes. I saw the devastation and pain in her eyes. We both cried. And it made me despise my father even more.

For over thirty years, I held unforgiveness and bitterness towards my father. Until the day I joined a small group and the leader spoke on the power of forgiveness. She mentioned that only by letting go and forgiving would I ever experience true freedom. That I should not wait for him to apologize, because by doing that I hold myself hostage to the very one who hurt me, and I place my freedom in his hands. The leader explained that forgiving the person who hurt you does not mean that you must reconcile with that person. She said, "It takes two to reconcile but only one to forgive."

To be honest, I did not want to forgive him. I wanted him to suffer miserably and feel pain like I had. Like my mother had. I wanted him to hurt like he hurt us. But one thing the small group leader said kept coming back to my memory—because I had been forgiven, I had to forgive. Even if he didn't deserve it. As long as I harbored unforgiveness, I was the one bound, not him. And if I continued to choose not to deal with it, it had the power to paralyze my ability to live, love, and be loved.

I decided this was something I must do if I was ever going to live a healthy, fulfilled life. I knew if I waited until I felt like it, I would never do it. So I picked up the phone and called him. Full of emotions and completely vulnerable, I simply said, "Dad, I just wanted to tell you that I forgive you and I love you, and from this day forward I will no longer hold unforgiveness in my heart towards you."

I immediately felt free from the enormous weight that I had carried for so many years. I knew this was a life-changing moment for me. But even though I felt immediate relief, forgiving my dad is something I will have to do for the rest of my life. When something triggers a memory or feelings of hate try to crowd my mind, I simply say a prayer of blessing for him, knowing that even though it may not change him, it changes me.

Who do you need to forgive?

I am certain that as soon as you read those words, a name immediately came to mind. The truth is, most of us have fallen victim to the words and deeds of others, causing indescribable pain and resentment. Abuse, neglect, betrayal, abandonment, and offensive words directed at us often lead to bitterness and unforgiveness that remain in our hearts long after they take place. When someone hurts us through words or actions, it may feel like unforgiveness is fair because they should have to pay for the offense. However, by holding on to unforgiveness, YOU end up being the one held captive, not the person who offended you.

In South America, the natives have discovered a very effective method of trapping monkeys. The plan is deceptively simple. They take a gourd and drill a hole just large enough for a monkey's hand to pass through. Next, they add extra weight to the gourd with sand or pebbles to weigh it down. Then, they put a piece of fruit inside and place the gourd where a monkey will find it.

Once the monkey discovers the gourd, it sticks its hand through the hole to get the fruit, but with the bait in its grasp, the monkey cannot get its hand back out. The hole is too small for the monkey's hand to pass through as long as it's holding the fruit. And the gourd is too heavy for the monkey to carry. Because the monkey will not let go of the bait, it becomes trapped, ultimately giving up its freedom by continuing to hold on.

It seems obvious that all the monkey needs to do is let go of the fruit and it can escape. But because it is not willing to let go, the monkey remains stuck. Bound by the thing it is unwilling to let go of.

It's easy for us to see how foolish it is to keep holding on to something that has the power to keep us trapped.

The monkey is acting out of instinct. It doesn't recognize the danger of grasping the bait—or the fact that doing so will have a dramatic impact on its future. Humans should be able to avoid falling into such a trap. We should be able to understand the danger of holding on to things that keep us bound.

Unfortunately, we sometimes choose to continue to hold on to unforgiveness and bitterness, even though it holds us in a constant state of captivity. The fact is, the monkey could have found freedom and lived an unbelievable life and experienced incredible successes. But because it was unwilling to let go of the bait, it remained trapped and eventually died that way. This decision sealed its fate. Only by letting go can we be free.

I need to tell you that the unforgiveness and bitterness you are holding onto could be keeping you from walking in your God-given purpose. Through my season of sickness, my eyes were opened to the blockages in my heart that had been built up from years of anger, resentment, and unforgiveness. I had to let go so God could fully use me in what He was calling me to do. Lysa TerKeurst says it best in her book, *Forgiving What You Can't Forget*, "It is necessary for you not to let pain rewrite your memories. And it's absolutely necessary not to let pain ruin your future."[5]

I was walking Auburn's campus one day when I came upon a single pecan on the ground. I bent over and picked it up and just stared at it. Then God spoke to me. He said, "Don't ever forget where I brought you from." I tucked the pecan in my pocket and knew I would use it to tell my story one day.

You see, the girl in the story was me. I didn't have a father that was there for me. I was the one who wished just once I had a dad that said he loved me and that I was beautiful. I was the one that looked forward to going to school because they gave free lunch. I was the one who picked up pecans to have something to eat.

What I experienced as a child and the struggles and hardships that I learned to fight through caused me to be dependent on God. Those hard moments prepared me for the big moments that were coming.

But the unforgiveness and bitterness I held in my heart led to physical, emotional, and mental pain that held me back from walking fully in my purpose. When I decided to fully let go and forgive, I was able to hear God more clearly and surrender to what God was leading me to do.

Whether you have had much or little. Whether things have come easy or always been a fight. Whether you are rich or poor. Have a perfect family or an imperfect one. Have the greatest education or very little. You have a purpose and a destiny that is calling out to you. But it will require you to let go of all unforgiveness and bitterness. The question is...will you answer it?

Takeaways:
- Your past does not define your future.
- Unforgiveness and bitterness can cause you to miss your destiny.
- Let go of unforgiveness so you can be free.

CHAPTER 5

Your Esther Moment

Why are you here?

When all three of my girls moved out of the house, I started asking myself that question. My identity had always been "Mom." I found myself questioning if my life had purpose anymore. I would fall in and out of depression and loneliness. And then one day it hit me. There are girls at Auburn University that are far away from their moms and most likely need a spiritual mama to guide them. I started co-leading a college girls' small group. I started mentoring college students. I could have never known that one small step into my purpose would lead to a movement on college campuses.

One of the most fulfilling things I get to do besides being a mom is to lead these college students. When UniteUS started, a door opened for me to be able to go into sororities and speak to the girls. My message is always the same:

"I get the honor of mentoring college students. One thing I realized early was that I can look at girls' Instagram pictures and they look amazing. But if I spend ten minutes with them, I learn very quickly that they are not amazing. As a matter of fact, most of the time behind those pictures is a lot of pain. Pain and anxiety that nobody knows about. But God doesn't want you full of anxiety, pain, isolation, loneliness, and depression. It's okay to not be okay...it's just not okay to stay there. On the other side of your pain is a great purpose. And God has a purpose for every single girl in this room."

The Story of Esther

Are you familiar with the story of Esther? Esther was an orphan. She grew up in the home of her cousin, Mordecai, who had a tremendous influence on her life. He taught her to respect her Jewish heritage and to always stay true to who she was. Esther grew into a beautiful, confident woman. She could have never anticipated the call that would be on her life and the tremendous impact her obedience would have on her people.

When the king of Persia became displeased with his wife, Vashti, he sought a new queen. Esther was taken to the royal palace, and King Ahasuerus loved her more than any of the other young women who were brought in. He was so delighted with her that he placed the royal crown on her head and declared her the new queen.

After hearing of an evil plot by Haman, the king's highest official, to eradicate all of the Jews, Esther's cousin, Mordecai, sent her a very direct message. He told her to approach the king and plead with him to protect her people. Esther knew that in doing so she would risk her life because the law stated that any man or woman who approached the king, unsummoned, would receive the death penalty—unless the king extended the gold scepter, allowing that person to live.

But Mordecai commanded her to not keep silent, emphasizing, "Relief and deliverance for the Jews will arise from another place, but you and your father's family will perish. And who knows but that you have come to your royal position for such a time as this?" (Esther 4:14).

Esther asked everyone to fast and to pray. She would go before the king. Unsummoned. And if she died, she died.

Esther revealed Haman's plot to the king. Enraged, the king had Haman killed and Mordecai promoted as his replacement. A new law was passed enabling the Jews to defend themselves, and consequently, they were spared from annihilation.

God's hand is not always immediately obvious in our lives. Whether it's the mundane day-to-day tasks or the occasional trial or even crisis, we easily wonder, "Why did this happen?" or "Where is God?" (Like Madi in the garage.) The book of Esther gives us the answer: He is there. He is orchestrating the events in our lives to bring about the purpose He desires.

Because Esther was placed in the palace "for such a time as this," we can trust God's timing for placing us in different situations. It's easy to struggle with timing, thinking that we are in the wrong place at the wrong time. But who knows? Maybe we are in the right place at the right time! What we can't see with our eyes, we must believe with our hearts. Every human being goes through difficulties where God seems to be absent. This is nothing new. Esther encourages us that even if we can't see God's hand, we should just be patient and step out in faith, believing we are in the right place.

Like Esther, God is preparing us for our own divine moments to lead us into our destiny. Moments that are a result of preparation, prayer, and obedience that propel us into God's ordained plan for our lives. God is calling you. He is calling you to step into your divine moment!

Below are five things to remember as you step out in faith:

1. Believe that God can use YOU.

    Esther had every reason to believe that she was not qualified for a destiny moment. Because of her Jewish heritage, she never should have even been allowed in the palace, much less in the king's court. But when God calls us, He makes a way even when it doesn't make sense.

If you feel God calling you to step into a destiny moment, take the step. If there is a dream, a mission, a path that He has put on your heart, but you've been putting it off, now is the time to take that step of faith.

2. Have the courage to say YES.
Esther had to think of her people and how it affected those she loved more than the fear that would hold her back. Her action or inaction greatly affected a nation. It took great courage to go against the king's orders and trust God to protect and save not only her but the entire Jewish people. How will your YES affect your life and others? What would the ripple effect of your YES lead to?

3. Use your VOICE.
Mordecai warned Esther that her silence would not only lead to the death of her people but would also lead to the death of herself and her family. Esther had a choice to make. She could speak out, or she could choose to remain silent. When you are given a moment to speak and use your voice to make an impact, don't allow fear or intimidation to hold you back. It's time to be bold and speak out. Who knows what your obedience will lead to?

4. Allow God to PROTECT you from your enemies. Haman's plan was to annihilate every Jew. Including Esther's family. But as God protected Esther in her obedience to Him, Haman hung on the very gallows that he planned to use against Esther's cousin, Mordecai. And Esther and Mordecai were both promoted. When we obey God, He takes vengeance on our enemies. We do not have to fight those battles.

5. Choose to OBEY, even when it doesn't make sense. Esther had to step out in faith and trust God, even when it didn't make sense. She knew what she had to do. Even if it cost her life. Sometimes God will call us to do things that go against culture or what is viewed as acceptable or normal. But what if your courage saves many lives or even shifts a nation? Will you trust God? Or fear man? Remember, God will give you the strength and boldness necessary to accomplish His great purpose.

God showed me a revelation. The Final Four, the stand for purity on *The Bachelor*, and prayer on Auburn's campus were all part of a bigger puzzle, and He was just connecting the pieces all lining up for the revival that is sweeping college campuses and this nation.

I'm nobody special. But I pray. A lot. God is looking for obedience. God is looking for people that will hear His voice and will say yes and obey.

God is calling you to step into something.

He is raising up modern-day Esthers that will rise up and use their voices to take back their campus, their city, their nation.

If you want to be part of that calling, say these declarations:

- I will no longer allow negative thoughts to have control over my mind or to stop me from what God is calling me to do.
- This will be a season when all things will be made new in my life.
- I will walk in my divine purpose and calling and fulfill my God-ordained destiny.
- I will no longer allow fear to stop me. I will walk in the courage of the Lord.

As you continue to make these declarations, trust God to give you boldness and influence, knowing that you were not born in this time by chance. It was part of a great plan to bring about a great purpose for such a time as this.

Rise Up and Fight

A few weeks after I had the vision for Unite, I started battling unexplainable depression. There was no apparent reason for this sudden depression. I felt like I was experiencing spiritual warfare at a greater level than I could cope with. I did not tell anyone, but I'm sure my family could tell something was off. I had no energy, no passion, no motivation, no joy. This was not like me. Surely there was a war raging for my mind and my calling that the enemy fought to take me out and stop what was coming. This went on for weeks until I had a complete breakdown. I have no idea what even triggered the breakdown, but it came hard and it came fast. I knew I could not stay that way. I knew I had to take unwanted steps to find myself again. I reached out to a very highly recommended counselor. I felt like God said after that first call, "You take care of Tonya, and I will take care of the vision." Wow!

I only engaged in three calls with the counselor. What I learned very quickly was that there were blockages in my heart that had grown year after year and were causing not only mental pain and anxiety but also physical and emotional pain. Most of this had to do with unforgiveness and letting go of the bitterness and resentment that had kept me trapped and imprisoned for so long.

I cannot explain to you how it happened. I made the decision to give it all to God. To forgive and to let go. When I did, He took over. Not only with me personally, but with the vision for Unite. I felt freedom like I never dreamed possible. I felt joy and passion again. And I had an urgency to move forward and move quickly. This urgency caused me to meet with one pastor, ministry leader, coach, and administrator after another. I was unstoppable. I knew what God wanted to do on our campus and that it was just the beginning of what was coming. We would later see more unprecedented salvations, deliverances, healings, baptisms, and connections than our nation had ever witnessed.

My word for the year, "Rise," came rushing to my memory. "Plan and lead an event. Lead students to freedom." God was opening doors and giving me the vision, but I had to be the one to RISE and obey. I had to step out in faith and take the steps to start. I had to speak the vision and fight to protect it and watch it unfold. (The saving of many!)

As I began to think through what Unite would look like, I had one memory or visual or message after another trigger what I felt needed to be the focus of the overall message or theme of these events—Truth and Hope. Truth about the consequences and effects of sexual sin and pornography (JP's message) and hope that there is freedom from anxiety, depression, suicidal thoughts, and addiction (Jennie's message). After Unite Auburn, I felt these same messages would be preached at every university across the nation.

It has been truly incredible to witness these students making decisions for salvation, rededication, freedom, and connection since our first event. The testimonies have been so powerful. Decades of addiction broken off, atheists giving their hearts to Jesus, suicidal thoughts broken, relationships restored, families healed, and so many that are now serving in their local church. It's all so beautiful.

This doesn't happen if someone doesn't rise up and obey. Just imagine the thousands that have experienced salvation, thousands baptized, thousands set free from sin and bondage, and thousands now serving in local churches. What if I had said no? Or let fear stop me? Or listened to the voices around me that said I wasn't qualified and this was too big for me?

I want to encourage you to rise up and be who God has called you to be. Allow your voice to be heard. And your influence to be felt. God has equipped you with everything you need to walk in the fullness of your calling. Don't hold back. You are an integral part of God's plan for your family and your area of influence.

God has anointed you for this time. He must be sickened by the sins of this generation. Sexual sin, addiction, pornography, human trafficking. How long will He sit back and allow this? Each of us has a responsibility to impact this generation. To help clean up what the enemy has made so dirty.

Thousands of students saved and baptized blows our minds. But should it? Why aren't hundreds around us getting baptized daily? Sin has become normal and accepted. We have become desensitized to this culture of sin and rebellion. God is calling us. He is calling you. Will you rise up and answer the call?

When Should You Step Out and Fight?

There may be times when we feel like we are in a fight but need to show restraint. Like Madison when she was on national television at *The Bachelor* finale. Even though fighting back may not have been wise in those moments, there are moments when we should and must stand up and fight. We should fight for our relationships. We should fight for our marriages. We should fight for our families. We should fight for our nation. We should fight for our values. We should fight for our worth. We should fight for our purity. We should fight for our faith. We should fight for what we believe in. Because if we do not fight to protect those things, then we will lose them.

It's time to stop spending time fighting small, insignificant battles that do not matter and rise up to fight the ones that do. In a world where everyone has forgotten what is truly valuable, we need to stand up and fight for what is important.

So, I ask you, where are the courageous leaders of our world today? Leaders who are confident, disciplined, and prepared? I believe it is time for you to rise up, recognize who you are, and embrace your moment.

Have you seen the movie *Wonder Woman*?⁶ It is a powerful story of a woman who realizes that she must go to battle and fight for those who could not fight for themselves.

As a young girl, Diana's (Wonder Woman's) mother knew that her daughter was destined to save her people. She knew the only way to protect her was to train her. To train her harder than any other. Until she was the strongest, wisest, and most skilled fighter. Training did not come easy. There were times Diana would take a hard blow, but she always got back up. Her trainer reminded her, "You are stronger than you think you are. Never let your guard down. You expect the battle to be fair. The battle is never fair." During the toughest times of training, Diana discovered her greatest strength. It wasn't anything anyone taught her. It was given to her at birth. It was what set her apart: her determination.

There was a pivotal moment in the movie when Diana knew she could no longer sit back and allow the injustice in the world to continue. She realized that all the training and all the preparation in her past had set her up for what was about to take place. This was her time. Time to take a stand. Time to fight. Time to make a difference, and she didn't hesitate. She tells her mother that she's ready. That she will not stand by any longer while innocent lives are lost. She boldly exclaims that if no one else will defend the world from the enemy, then she must. That she is willing to fight for those who cannot fight for themselves. Her mother reminds her that if she leaves, she may never come back. I love Diana's response, "But who will I be if I stay?"

Later, when Diana reached the battlefield, she saw a desperate woman begging for help while clutching her starving infant. The lady described the horror and suffering her family had faced. It was a defining moment for Diana. She knew the enemy was on the other side, but she refused to stay back. The soldiers told her it was impossible, that she could not save everyone in this war. She boldly responded, "It's what I'm going to do."

She put on her battle suit and proceeded to go in the direction of the enemy. She did not walk. She ran. She ran toward the enemy, and when he fired his darts, she didn't stop. She didn't back down. She didn't turn back. She kept advancing. She continued toward the enemy, and she took each of them down one by one until they were defeated. She was shot at. Outnumbered. And fought with fewer weapons. But she used what she had, and she won. Once she made up her mind that she was going to battle, nothing would stop her. What she was fighting to protect was more important. She kept her mission at the forefront of her mind. It motivated her to keep going, even when she was beaten down and tired.

In today's world, we can no longer stand by and watch innocent lives be destroyed by injustice. We must be willing to fight for those who cannot fight for themselves. Who will we be if we sit back and allow injustice to continue? It's time for us to suit up and go to battle. To make up our minds that nothing is going to stop us because some things are worth fighting to protect.

I want to challenge you to use your voice. Use your position. Use your skills. Use whatever you have to speak out and make a difference in this moment in time. When you are called to fight, fight.

Takeaways:
- You are made for more.
- You are stronger than you think.
- Who will you be if you do not answer the call?

CHAPTER 6

See Me

On a recent trip to visit my youngest daughter, Mary Mykal, I encountered the worst thunderstorm I had ever driven in on my way home. A monsoon. I couldn't see in any direction, and I doubted other drivers could either, so I flipped on my hazard lights, internally screaming, "Please see me! I need you to see me!" As I was navigating my way through the sheets of rain, I had an overwhelming epiphany. It occurred to me that others are crying out to us, "See me! I need you to see me! See me for who I am, not who you want me to be. See me in my good times and my low times. See me when I win; see me when I lose. See me when I'm insecure, sad, disappointed, confused, overwhelmed, and feeling hopeless. I need you to see me."

Every one of us has challenges set before us that we must face and learn to conquer, but as women we face some of the strongest attacks—attacks to our identity, worth, body image, mental health, and purpose. To fight against these unique attacks, we desperately need others who can exemplify strength, encourage daily, and steward us towards success.

So how do we help build others up to fight back against even the greatest lies that might stand in the way of discovering their destiny?

Mary Mykal went on a mission trip to the Middle East in the summer of 2023. When I picked her up from the airport, she started telling me one story after another. She told me how she watched as little children worked in brick factories all day. She told me how families worked in these factories day and night for decades. They weren't allowed to be sick. And if they didn't meet their quota, their wives were raped in front of them. If they didn't work to meet expectations, they were beaten until bones were broken. She talked about how the families that were stuck in this slavery didn't know any other way. They had accepted this as their lot in life. They had been stuck for so long that they didn't even realize freedom was a possibility. That's why Mary and the team went. To purchase their freedom. While they were there, they were able to pay the debts for fifty-nine families and celebrate their freedom. Truly amazing!

While Mary was there, I got a voice text from the director of the ministry. He said, "Tonya, I had to call and tell you what just happened. We had the privilege of meeting with a family to tell them that they would no longer be held as slaves in this factory and that we would be paying their debt. One of their daughters had severe mental health issues. So badly that she could not speak, did not communicate with others, and could not sit in the sun." He took a long pause—I knew he was weeping. Then he continued, "I looked over and saw Mary Mykal sitting under a tree with the daughter. She was holding her hands and looking directly into her eyes. She was not verbally speaking, but I knew she was communicating to this precious girl, saying, 'I see you. I am here with you. You are seen. And you are loved.'" He said it was the most special moment of the entire trip.

I shared this story with my small group. I have shared it with many sororities. I challenge them to look around. See the girls around them that are struggling. See the girls that are hurting. Anxious. Overlooked. Broken. Alone.

In 2021, when I was so sick with Covid, it seemed everyone else was going on with their lives and there were many times it felt extremely lonely. It was easy to feel forgotten or like I was a burden to my family and friends. It was in these moments that God really used my middle daughter, Mallory, to remind me that I was seen, even though I was so sick. She stayed with me as often as she could. She prayed for me and took care of me. When I was finally able to get out of the house again, she would go on long walks with me and drive me anywhere I wanted to go. We would have picnics in the park, and she would just sit with me for hours if I wanted her to.

Mallory sacrificed her own happiness to make sure I was okay. She "saw me" in one of the darkest moments of my life.

You never forget when people "see you."

I believe God is calling each of us to see those around us no matter where we are. We never know how a word, a hug, a kind gesture, or a smile can change someone's day or even their destiny.

How Do I Truly Make a Difference?

How do I help other people with what God has given me? How do I walk out my purpose in confidence? How can I make a difference?

You were put on this earth to add value. Not just take and get all that you can. You are called to contribute and make a difference. You need to know that you have something in you that someone else needs. The gifts, strengths, and dreams inside of you that set you apart and make you unique are not just for you; they are for others. Your strengths and gifts were given to you so that you could help others and add value to the people around you.

Trying to figure out what you are good at and what you are passionate about will come with a whole lot of trial and error. Figuring out what you will do with your life can come with a lot of risks and steps of faith. That can seem like a lot of pressure.

Sometimes it takes a lot of faith and stepping out of our comfort zone and even failing in order to discover what we were put on this earth for and how we can make a difference. It took me a while before I truly discovered and began to walk out what I felt purposed to do with my life. I learned a lot along the way about who I am and what makes me feel a sense of fulfillment. If you find yourself wondering if there is more out there, I challenge you: stop thinking and start doing. If it sounds interesting, fun, exciting, and you have a peace and good feeling about trying it—go for it. You don't want to get to the end of your life and feel, "I could have done more. I could have spoken out more. I could have given more." Start now! You were put on this earth to make a contribution. I know many of us ask ourselves, "But how do I do that?"

First, we need to eliminate the non-essentials: distractions, bad relationships, and busyness. If we don't eliminate the non-essentials, it will be hard for us to live out our full potential and purpose. Take a second and look over your day-to-day life. What is getting your focus and attention? Are you spending most of your time on social media? Netflix? Taking naps? Spending time with people that you know aren't good for you?

Listening to music that alters how you view yourself and others? Do you find yourself by the end of the day wondering what you did and what you accomplished? Do you find yourself admiring or envying the people around you who seem to be full of purpose, focus, and discipline? Then it is time to get rid of these non-essentials, the things in your life that do not add any value to you or those around you. You can only give away what you have within. So, taking time to make sure you are being filled with the right things and spending your time doing those things that add value to you is important.

Distractions are all around us. Distractions we always have with us. We carry that phone around everywhere we go. We pull up one app, and before we know it, we have spent hours of our day watching videos that aren't adding any value to us. Have you ever been around someone who is easily distracted? You are trying to tell them a story, and they are constantly checking their phone, people-watching, or looking away. It is annoying. Personally, I don't enjoy spending time with people like this. If I am giving you something that is valuable to me—my time—I expect it to be valued in return.

If we find it so annoying when other people do this to us, why do we constantly do this to ourselves? You have something valuable inside of you, and you can't afford to treat it any less than that. Take some time to evaluate what those distractions are for you and the moments that you easily give in to them. Awareness is always key—something I have continued to stress throughout this book. Only through becoming aware of when you are easily distracted can you fix the issue of being distracted. You have too much purpose inside of you to be lying around and wasting it!

Bad relationships are also another non-essential for you to walk out your purpose and destiny. The wrong relationships will not only distract you but will also detract value from you. We have to be careful with whom we spend our time. Again, your time and your life are valuable. If you are picky about your clothes, your makeup, and your food—things that have no effect on your purpose—you should be even more picky with those who can add to or detract from who you are and who you are called to be. One of my favorite quotes is by Steve Maraboli: "If you hang out with chickens you are going to cluck and if you hang out with eagles, you are going to fly."[7] Whoever you surround yourself with the most will start to affect how you view yourself, what you see for yourself, and what you believe about yourself. If you let someone else define your life, they will. And if you don't decide how you want to live your life, the rest of the world will decide it for you. Do you have people in your life that you know do not add any value to who you are? Begin to distance yourself from those people. You can't afford to have the wrong crowd around you for where God wants to take you.

Busyness. Have you noticed that when we ask the question, "How are you?" to people, oftentimes the response back is "Good, just so busy." Busyness can become an excuse or a lazy habit. What I mean by that is busyness is not always equated with productiveness. Just because you are busy does not mean you are being productive or effective. I don't mean to offend if you are the person who typically responds this way, but I do want to challenge you to change your verbiage and thought process when it comes to busyness.

Why do you think we always call homework that doesn't have anything to do with our tests and projects "busywork?" We call it busy because it isn't actually adding value but rather just something for us to do. Instead of seeing your day, your season, your life as busy, start reframing your mindset and training your mindset to see it as focused, productive, or purposeful. You don't have time for busywork. Time is ticking. We have to prioritize what is important and valuable to us so that we don't get distracted from what our attention should be on. I know some seasons are fuller than others, but don't allow busyness to become an excuse to not do what you are destined to do.

Now that we have eliminated the non-essentials, we are ready to discover our purpose and start making a difference! There is no time to waste. You only get one life. There are not any re-dos. So, do it right! Start the process now, whatever it takes to figure out why you were put on this earth. It's not too late. You're not too old. You're also not too young to start making a difference. Fifteen, twenty, fifty, eighty—doesn't matter. If you are still breathing, there is still time to learn more, discover more, do more.

Takeaways:
- You are seen and you are loved.
- "See" others.
- You were put on this earth to make a difference.

CHAPTER 7

Step Into Your Purpose

Life is like a race. Sometimes we are running full on with joy and purpose, and sometimes we are on the sidelines watching everyone else run their race. Maybe you are living your best life. Running full-on in your purpose. Or maybe you are the one that feels unseen on the sidelines. Either way, you have a responsibility—either go find the person sitting under the tree and help her get back in the race or pick yourself back up and start running again. You are not meant to be stuck, isolated, and alone with no purpose. God put something special inside of you, but it's up to you to tap into it. You were created on purpose for a purpose and are meant to live that out!

Purpose motivates your life and produces passion. Nothing can give you more of a thrill, rush of excitement, and fullness like clear purpose. Knowing you are wanted, needed, and valuable gives you a sense of confidence and motivation. You look forward to waking up the next morning and getting a start to another day. When life has purpose, you can endure almost anything; without it, nothing is endurable.

What is purpose? I believe purpose is when your gifts meet your passions. It's when you combine what makes you the happiest with what you are the best at. And until you learn that God-given purpose, you are going to be forever searching for it in all of the wrong things, constantly leaving you unsatisfied and depressed.

Ephesians 2:10 (NIV) says, "For we are God's masterpiece. He has created us anew in Christ Jesus, so we can do the good things he planned for us long ago." This verse in Ephesians shows us that God had the thing for us to do first, and then He made us. There was purpose on your life and for your life before you were ever even born. God didn't make you out of experimentation or curiosity. No, He had a plan and purpose for you from the start, and He designed you intentionally to walk out that purpose! This verse also shows us that first you have to know who you are—you need to be confident in your identity and your self-worth. Then you will be able to walk out the purpose He has planned for you. It is important to know the order here. First, you need to know who you fully are in Christ before you can fully tap into the purpose and potential that is on your life! If you don't have anything within, you don't have anything to give.

Do you have any idea how old Moses was when God told him to lead the Israelites out of Egypt? He was eighty years old! David was fifteen when God sent him to defeat Goliath! I was fifty years old when God gave me the vision for Unite. My daughter, Madison, was twenty-three when she wrote her first book. Sadie Robertson was eighteen when she preached her first sermon.

We all have a purpose and a destiny. Some look very different than others. But it's important that we hear and obey God when He calls us to step out.

How Do I Discover My Calling?

How do I discover my calling? How do I know if I am walking out my purpose? Am I in God's will?

Your purpose is to love God and love people. Simple. That is my purpose too. That is what God put inside all of us. But our specific calling is going to look different for each of us. Because we are all so different. You have gifts, strengths, and passions that are unique to you. Your calling is a combination of passion and gifting. What are you most passionate about? What gifts, strengths, and abilities do you have that set you apart? Ask yourself, where have I already been successful and fruitful that other people have confirmed? What do I enjoy doing the most? What gets me out of bed in the morning? What makes me the angriest?

One thing that I have learned is that if you serve wholeheartedly where you are, commit to growing every day, and trust God in the process, your calling will find you! For me, that looked like giving my all to whatever season I was in and using the gifts and the influence God gave me. When I had young children, I spent a lot of time playing with dolls and watching children's movies and going to the park and taking them to ballet lessons and to church events. During that time, I was also a teacher, so I invested in my students and coworkers. When my daughters got older, I spent a lot of time at their basketball games and cheering events. I was "all in" Mom!

After my girls left the house and began college and started careers, I started leading a college girls' small group and volunteering at a children's home. As I was leading these amazing girls and providing respite care for these babies whose moms were in prison, I discovered that I am purposed to do two things: empower students, meeting them where they are but helping them get to where they could be, and fighting for those who can't fight for themselves. I didn't know exactly how it would play out and what it would look like, but I knew that was why I was put on this earth.

Now, I use my purpose through Unite events, speaking and writing, sharing my faith, offering hope and grace to those searching, and challenging and empowering others to see all that they are so they can rise up and become all they were meant to be. That is what I challenge you with. Each season of your life matters, but each season will most likely look different, some more challenging than others. But in each season, there is something God wants to teach you and a way that He wants to use you.

How Can I Hear From God?

Listen.

My daughters, the students I mentor, and younger moms often ask me the question, "How can I hear from God?" I would say to anyone who asks this that the best way to hear from God is to silence the noise around you and LISTEN.

I've always been intentional in spending time with God. I pray a lot. After I got really sick in 2021, I had health issues that caused me to become isolated from people. I would spend most of my days taking long prayer walks. It was during these walks, alone with God, that I learned to hear His voice. I started seeing visions and having revelations. The more time I spent with God, the more I would hear from Him.

Takeaways:
- You were created on purpose for a purpose. Discover it and walk in it!
- Your calling is a combination of passion and gifting.
- To hear from God, you must LISTEN!

CHAPTER 8

Pain to Purpose

I don't often remember my dreams, but when they are so clear that I cannot forget them, I get up and write them down. In this one particular dream, I was running around trying to help make sure my family was all okay. I kept hearing my youngest, Mary Mykal, calling for me, but I couldn't find her. I was running around frantically, trying to figure out where she was. When I found her, she was in a hospital bed hooked up to machines and reaching for me. She was desperately calling for me. I will never forget the look on her face as she begged for me to help her. I could not get to her. It felt like a spiritual pull for her life.

On January 27, 2022, I got a call at 2:00 a.m. The officer on the other line said, "Mrs. Prewett, I am calling to let you know that I have your daughter, Mary Mykal. I have arrested her for driving under the influence. I will be taking her to the county jail, where she will stay the night. You will be able to pick her up tomorrow at 2:00 p.m. Oh, and one last thing, Mrs. Prewett—I truly believe if I had not pulled your daughter over, she would not be alive right now."

Talk about a gut-wrenching call. I never went to sleep that night. The "what-ifs" consumed my mind. What if Mary is being abused? What if she is terrified? What if she becomes suicidal? What if she is calling for me, but I cannot help her? It was the hardest moment of my life.

When my husband and I picked her up from the county jail the next day, Mary's face was swollen and red from crying all night. I could feel her shame and humiliation. I could feel the guilt. She would have rather been anywhere but looking into the eyes of her mother and father. But what I said to her in that moment was, "Mary, I have never loved you more than I do right now." I held her for a very long time and just thanked God over and over for her life.

Before I tell you what came next, I want to share Mary's journal entry ten months later:

Why am I alive?

January 27, 2022

I'm sitting in a jail cell asking myself this question. This wasn't me trying to figure out the next steps for my purpose following the arrest. This was me trying to find a good enough reason to want to wake up the next day. Would anyone care if I were gone? I'm a disappointment. The things I've done are unforgivable. I can't come back from this. How will anyone love me anymore? I can't imagine what my parents and sisters are thinking of me right now. Do I even belong in the family I'm in? They do all of the right things while I do all of the wrong things. My friends tell me my actions are okay, but did I let their approval lead me here? What small choices led me on a path that ended here? Why did that cop stop me at 1:30 a.m.? Why didn't he just let me die?

In this exact moment, I believe Satan thought he had won my life. Little did he know that an hour later my whole life perspective would be changed. One of the women in the jail had been comforting me after what was realistically the worst day of my life. She looked at me and said, "Mary, look around this room. You don't belong here." Then she laughed, and we carried on a conversation. But those words stuck with me. Although some of the women in there had done unexplainable, horrible things, at the end of the day, my mistakes led me to be in the same place as them. I believe this was God showing me what hell would be like if I didn't wake up.

November 4, 2022

 Sitting in my room in awe of what God has done in my life in such a quick time. Why am I alive? I'm alive to show others that there is absolutely nothing in this world that can bring fulfillment or satisfaction. The only thing it brought me was shame, guilt, regret, unforgiveness, indulgence, discontentment, and darkness. But today I'm free of every lie and hold the devil had placed on me. I'm happier and more joyful than I would have ever imagined. I feel purposeful and I love my life. It took me getting to the absolute lowest low in order for me to wake up and see that there was more to this life than temporary pleasures.

 I'm here to say that you don't have to get to that breaking point. This life is temporary. Eternity is waiting for us. It's our choice to choose which way we want to spend it. I truly believe that if I had died on January 27, 2022, I would not have gone to heaven. But on January 27, 2023, I will start my first day of a five-month-long discipleship training school that will train me to go to other nations and spread the gospel. In one year, I will go from an inmate to a disciple. If He can do that for me in 365 days, I can only imagine what He is going to do for you.

One week after Mary Mykal walked out of that jail cell, she joined a Freedom small group through our church. This small group shifted her life. At the end of each small group semester, there is a Freedom conference that is saturated in prayer. Mary told us how one of the leaders looked her in the eyes before praying and said, "Mary, I see you. I love you. And you have a great purpose." Then she prayed a powerful prayer over her future. That was a game-changer. Mary started meeting with her sorority sisters, one after another, sharing her testimony and the good news of Jesus. She would walk them through scripture and disciple them. She started leading her own small group with college students. This created a deep desire for discipleship training, which led her to YWAM in Kona, Hawaii, for a semester. She has been on two mission trips and experienced two missions training programs.

It's time for us to rise up and cancel the devil's assignment over our children, over this generation. It doesn't matter your age or what season of life you are in. God can use you to make an impact on those around you. He is looking for people who will step up, speak out, use their past pain for a purpose, and PRAY.

When you think God is doing nothing, you are wrong. He is writing your story. Orchestrating the events and chapters of your life. It's all part of the manuscript of a full story.

Remember the story of Madi calling from the garage? She thought God had forgotten her. Overlooked her. But God was actually preparing her. He was using those moments of pain as preparation to bring about a greater story than she could have ever imagined. A husband. A platform. A book. A message. Revival. So much more.

Takeaways:
- Your pain can propel you into your greatest purpose.
- God is writing your story.

CHAPTER 9

The Power of Prayer

As I lead into the last chapter of the book, I cannot end without emphasizing the power of prayer. None of the things that happened over the course of the last five years of my life happened without prayer. Prayer precedes a move of God. Prayer precedes miracles. Prayer precedes something BIG happening. And prayer will be what ushers in the greatest harvest of souls before the return of Jesus!

I will spend the rest of this chapter telling you stories of how prayer has shifted things in the life of my family. You have already heard about the Final Four. You have already heard about Madi's unlikely journey on *The Bachelor*. You have already heard the miraculous story of how God healed me when I was so close to death. Let me encourage you with a few more.

This story may seem small to you, but small steps of obedience lead to BIG acts of God. Early in our careers, Chad and I worked at a private school in Mobile, Alabama. Chad coached basketball, and I taught second grade at Faith Academy. We were heavily involved in a local church, where I led women's events and children and adult dramas. Our girls were involved in sports and all the church dramas. To us, it was all so perfect. When Chad got a call to consider a job at Lee-Scott Academy in Auburn, Alabama, we knew he had to at least consider it. But we were all hoping it wouldn't work out.

He went in for an interview, and the headmaster made an offer that was hard to ignore. So, we started praying. I went with him to the second interview. When we left to head back to Mobile, we prayed for God to give us a sign that we would know without a doubt that He was leading us to Auburn. After we prayed, I took out a bag of peanut M&M's and nervously ate almost the whole bag. Chad does not like peanut M&M's, but for some strange reason he asked if he could have some. I poured what was left into his hand. Two M&M's—one orange and one blue. We packed our bags and moved to Auburn.

That might seem like a crazy story to you, but what if we had not obeyed in that moment? Final Four. Bachelor. Revival. When we pray, God answers. We have to listen and obey.

Madi started dating this guy when she was in the ninth grade. He was a senior. I didn't feel good about it. I remember not being able to sleep one night and thinking I needed to pray for Madi. I walked into her room at 2:00 a.m. and found her phone at the foot of her bed.

God said, "Pick it up and read the text messages." I thought, "Even if I tried, I don't know her password. No joke—when I picked it up, the phone went straight to a message without asking for a password. The message was from the guy she was dating. It read, "I cannot wait until next week when you turn sixteen and start driving! We will get more alone time."

I'm pretty sure I threw the phone and went straight to my prayer closet. I prayed, "God! Make Madison so sick of this guy that the very thought of him makes her sick!" The next week, she got sick and missed a few days of school. After returning to school, I asked her about her boyfriend. She said, "Ew! I broke up with him! The very thought of him makes me sick!" Okay, God! I prayed specifically, and He answered just what I prayed for! What if I hadn't prayed? Look at Madi today! Married to the man of her dreams and running in her purpose!

In 2018, one of the Auburn University men's basketball coaches was under investigation for some legal issues. The threat that the coaches were hearing was that all current staff would be fired by Tuesday. Why would we freak out? We freaked out. I started leading Jericho marches around Auburn's Basketball Arena. I, along with other coaches' wives, joined in the march. We walked around Auburn's arena seven times, while quoting scripture and praying. We declared that none of the coaches would lose their jobs. On Tuesday, not one of the coaches lost their job.

I remember a couple of years ago, standing on the balcony of the condo we were renting in Auburn while our house was being built and praying, "God, would You save and heal the students at Auburn University? Would You send revival to Auburn's campus? Would You draw these students to You?" I could have never dreamed two years ago what the results of those prayers would look like. But God heard them. And He didn't stop at Auburn. He far exceeded what I asked for.

Something bigger is coming.

I believe the prayer that led to the revival that is moving across college campuses will continue and usher in the return of Jesus. It won't stop.

Takeaways:
- Prayer moves God.
- Small steps of obedience lead to big acts of God.

CHAPTER 10

The King Is Coming!

My friend and I decided we were going to start a podcast together. I started writing down possible titles for our podcast name. I had about twenty written down. One of the titles had the word "Crown" in it.

As we prayed about the title for our podcast, the strangest thing started happening. I couldn't go anywhere that I didn't see crowns. It was happening so much that I started taking pictures of the crowns so people would understand. It may seem strange to some, but that is how God speaks to me. By repeating Himself. It's His way of getting my attention. First the roses. Then Exodus 33. Then the crowns.

I decided to hire someone to help us with the launch of our podcast. Out of the twenty names, she told us that she thought we had to use the title with "crown" in it.

We decided to name our podcast "Pick Up Your Crown!"

Our podcast kept getting pushed back due to crazy life schedules. But the "crowns" kept coming. I would see them multiple times a day. I was thinking, "God, You have my attention!"

On a trip with my youngest daughter, Mary, to visit my middle daughter, Mallory, in Nashville, I had a strong revelation from the Lord. I told my girls, "I think the reason I keep seeing crowns is because God is telling me, 'The King is coming.'" We didn't think much more about it and went on with our day. Crowns everywhere. It was getting comical. A couple of days later, my mother sent me a text message saying she had just met the cutest guy and Mallory should meet him. She sent me a photo. The guy was wearing a t-shirt with a CROWN, and underneath it were the words THE KING IS COMING. I was sure God was trying to tell me something. A week later, I clicked on YouTube to look for a song, and an interview with a guy I had never listened to popped up. One of the first things he said was, "The King is coming!"

I started praying—asking God what all of this meant and why He was going out of His way to tell me this. He said, "I am coming soon; tell my people."

Sleep did not come easy. I started having very intense dreams about future Unite events. In every dream, I was desperately working on plans for the event. This went on for a few weeks. I would wake up in the middle of the night during the dreams with no full clarity on what was missing in the planning.

I have always slept with a sound machine for as long as I can remember. I keep the sound on *white noise*. I have never changed it in ten years. On Thursday, June 6, I woke up at exactly 3:00 a.m. to the sound of a clock ticking. I was so confused, as I do not have any clocks in my room. I picked up my phone and discovered that it was my sound machine. It had changed from *white noise* to a *ticking clock*. I had not touched my phone and was alone in the bed that night. "The King is Coming" kept playing over and over in my head. Again, I wondered why God was trying so hard to make sure I heard this message.

Then it occurred to me. God has given me an open door through Unite to spread the word across college campuses. I have been given the message and the means to deliver it. The King is coming. Soon.

Unite Auburn. Unite other college campuses. Unite the nation. We've seen it happen at Auburn. We are continuing to see it happen on other college campuses. I have seen a greater gathering where thousands of students will gather on the White House lawn in Washington, D.C. Where students, along with national leaders, pastors, and coaches will join together for prayer and worship for our nation.

This vision all started with prayer. It will continue with prayer, and prayer will make things happen that can only be explained by God.

Afterword

As I was writing this book, I was contacted by a couple of book agents. I was so excited that an agent would want to promote this story. I started having conversations with one of the agents, and it all felt right. Then we started talking timeline. He said it could be up to two years before the book would be published. I was feeling the same urgency that I felt for Unite Auburn and explained that I would need the book to be published by the summer of 2025. I went on to explain that I kept having this feeling that my book would come out around the same time that a film would come out about the revival sweeping college campuses. He listened but still assured me that it would most likely be two years.

I decided I would need to find another agent or publisher that could move faster. After an initial call with Trilogy Publishing, I knew this was the direction I needed to go. On February 5, 2025, I signed a contract with Trilogy Publishing, and on that same day I was contacted by a major news source that asked to do a documentary film on the story of Unite by summer of 2025!

I recently watched the movie "Braveheart." In the movie, Mel Gibson played the part of a Scottish warrior (William Wallace) who rose to fight against the king of England. I thought about this. What causes a person to rise up and fight? We fight for what we believe in. I believe Gen Z is worth fighting for. Our families are worth fighting for. Truth is worth fighting for. Our nation is worth fighting for.

You, too, are called to make a difference. To rise up and fight for what's important to you. The time is now. He's coming soon!

7   Maraboli, Steve. 2013. *Unapologetically You: Reflections on Life and the Human Experience*. Port Washington, N.Y.: A Better Today.

Endnotes

1. Vawser, Lana. 2014. Review of THERE IS a RESOUNDING SOUND from HEAVEN "WILL YOU TRUST ME and MY DIRECTION?" Lana Vawser Ministries. July 24, 2014. https://lanavawser.com/there-is-a-resounding-sound-from-heaven-will-you-trust-me-and-my-direction/.

2. "TD Jakes. Treasures in Darkness. Watch Online Sermons." 2025. https://sermons.love/td-jakes/5739-td-jakes-treasures-in-darkness.html.

3. Prewett, Madison. 2021. *Made for This Moment: Standing Firm with Strength, Grace, and Courage.* Grand Rapids: Zondervan Books.

4. Kasi, Lemmons, dir. 2019. *Harriet.* [Motion Picture] Focus Features.

5. TerKeurst, Lysa. 2020. *Forgiving What You Can't Forget.* Thomas Nelson, 18.

6. Jenkins, Patty, dir. 2017. *Wonder Woman* [Motion Picture]. Directed by Patty Jenkins. Warner Bros. Pictures.

www.ingramcontent.com/pod-product-compliance
Lightning Source LLC
LaVergne TN
LVHW021945230925
821792LV00018B/1900